Narratives in Social Science Research

INTRODUCING QUALITATIVE METHODS provides a series of volumes which introduce qualitative research to the student and beginning researcher. The approach is interdisciplinary and international. A distinctive feature of these volumes is the helpful student exercises.

One stream of the series provides texts on the key methodologies used in qualitative research. The other stream contains books on qualitative research for different disciplines or occupations. Both streams cover the basic literature in a clear and accessible style, but also cover the 'cutting edge' issues in the area.

SERIES EDITOR
David Silverman (Goldsmiths College)

EDITORIAL BOARD
Michael Bloor (University of Wales, Cardiff)
Barbara Czarniawska (Göteborg University)
Norman Denzin (University of Illinois, Champaign)
Barry Glassner (University of Southern California)
Jaber Gubrium (University of Missouri)
Anne Murcott (South Bank University)
Jonathan Potter (Loughborough University)

TITLES IN SERIES
Doing Conversation Analysis
Paul ten Have

Using Foucault's Methods
Gavin Kendall and Gary Wickham

The Quality of Qualitative Research
Clive Seale

Qualitative Evaluation
Ian Shaw

Researching Life Stories and Family Histories
Robert L. Miller

Categories in Text and Talk
Georgia Lepper

Focus Groups in Social Research
Michael Bloor, Jane Frankland, Michelle Thomas, Kate Robson

Qualitative Research Through Case Studies
Max Travers

Gender and Qualitative Methods
Helmi Jarviluoma, Pirkko Moisala and Anni Vilkko

Methods of Critical Discourse Analysis
Ruth Wodak and Michael Meyer

Qualitative Research in Social Work
Ian Shaw and Nick Gould

Qualitative Research in Information Systems
Michael D. Myers and David Avison

Researching the Visual
Michael Emmison and Philip Smith

Qualitative Research in Education
Peter Freebody

Using Documents in Social Research
Lindsay Prior

Doing Research in Cultural Studies
Paula Saukko

Qualitative Research in Sociology: An Introduction
Amir B. Marvasti

Criminological Research
Lesley Noaks and Emma Wincup

Narratives in Social Science Research

Barbara Czarniawska

Los Angeles | London | New Delhi
Singapore | Washington DC

First published 2004
Reprinted 2008, 2009, 2011, 2012

 SAGE Publications Ltd
1 Oliver's Yard
55 City Road
London EC1Y 1SP

SAGE Publications Inc.
2455 Teller Road
Thousand Oaks, California 91320

SAGE Publications India Pvt Ltd
B 1/I 1, Mohan Cooperative Industrial Area
Mathura Road
New Delhi 110 044

SAGE Publications Asia-Pacific Pte Ltd
3 Church Street
#10-04 Samsung Hub
Singapore 049483

British Library Cataloguing in Publication data

A catalogue record for this book is available
from the British Library

ISBN 978 0 7619 4194 1
ISBN 978 0 7619 4195 8 (pbk)

Library of Congress Control Number 2003109257

Typeset by C&M Digitals (P) Ltd., Chennai, India
Printed in Great Britain by the MPG Books Group

Contents

Foreword

David Silverman

Qualitative research began as a 'naturalistic' genre (see Gubrium and Holstein, 1997). In this sense, the anthropologists and the sociologists of the 1930s working at the University of Chicago set out to document the 'raw' world as it was lived and experienced by its subjects. 'Naturalism' produced rich and compelling accounts of various aspects and forms of everyday life. However, in the second half of the century, many qualitative researchers became suspicious about the claims of this genre.

For some, the naturalists failed to recognize sufficiently the gendered and socially and ethnically stratified character of the world – and of their own writing about it (Denzin and Lincoln, 2000). For others, an observer's ability to see regularities in 'everyday life' depends upon a complex body of linguistically mediated interactions that demand analysis. Discourse analysis (DA) and conversation analysis (CA) grasp this point and, in doing so, they offer a cumulative body of empirical work that richly documents how interaction is put together in real time by its participants (see Silverman, 2001: Ch. 6).

Narrative analysis (NA) shares this linguistic turn with DA and CA. Arguably, NA has had a broader appeal to qualitative researchers than either DA or CA perhaps because it appears to fit better into quite conventional research studies. For instance, while CA and (to an increasing extent) DA tend to favor 'naturally occurring' data, narrative researchers often work with open-ended interviews. In doing so, they have provided their mainstream colleagues with a helpful means of reading sense into their interviews – still the most preferred form of qualitative data.

Barbara Czarniawska has been foremost among those scholars working on narratives (see Czarniawska, 1997; 1998; 1999a; 2003b). Indeed, her work encompasses many of the themes that concern qualitative researchers at the beginning of the twenty-first century: the turn to language, the recognition of gender and power relations, and the postmodern concern with how we narrate our own research.

Narratives in Social Science Research is enriched by Barbara's long interest in the subject, documented by several publications and graduate courses on the topic that she has taught in many countries. It is intended as a textbook for social science researchers who are interested in using a narrative approach: final-year undergraduates and graduate students but also researchers who decide to explore new perspectives. It can be used in anthropology, social psychology, sociology, management, economics, political sciences, cultural geography, and cultural studies. It will work effectively both as a main text in a course in narrative methods and as a supplementary text in general methodology courses.

The book begins with a brief historical sketch of the relationship between the humanities and social sciences and the recent rapprochement between the two as expressed in the interest in the narrative. It ends with listing possible reasons for using a narrative approach. The structure of the main part of the book helpfully follows the chronology of a research project. It demonstrates how a narrative approach can be applied in fieldwork (observing how stories are made, collecting stories, evoking narratives), how such collected or produced narratives can be read (interpretation, structural analysis, close readings), and ends by exploring the analogy between social science writing and other texts. Most chapters have one or more exercises and a helpful further reading list. A particularly helpful point is that examples in all the chapters are taken from many different branches of social sciences and draw upon the author's own research.

As editor of this series, *Introducing Qualitative Methods,* it is a pleasure to welcome a scholar of Barbara Czarniawska's distinction. I have no doubt that this book will be of great value to both students and researchers.

David Silverman
London

Acknowledgments

I would like to thank the participants of the graduate course given at Göteborg University in the Fall of 2002 for the patience and attention they gave this book's first draft: Kems o. Adu-Gyan, Maria Bolin, Dorit Christensen, Andreas Diedrich, Malin Gawell, Märta Hammarström, Patrik Johansson, Tina Karrbom, Elisabeth Ravenshorst, Nicklas Salomonson, Anna Maria Szczepanska, Kristian Wasen, and Cecilia Åkerblom.

1

The 'Narrative Turn' in Social Studies

A brief history

One of the most quoted utterances proclaiming the central role of narratives in social life comes from Roland Barthes (1915–1980), the French semiologist and literary critic:

> The narratives of the world are numberless. Narrative is first and foremost a prodigious variety of genres, themselves distributed amongst different substances – as though any material were fit to receive man's stories. Able to be carried by articulated language, spoken or written, fixed or moving images, gestures, and the ordered mixture of all these substances; narrative is present in myth, legend, fable, tale, novella, epic, history, tragedy, drama, comedy, mime, painting … stained glass windows, cinema, comics, news item, conversation. Moreover, under this almost infinite diversity of forms, narrative is present in every age, in every place, in every society; it begins with the very history of mankind and there nowhere is nor has been a people without narrative. All classes, all human groups, have their narratives … Caring nothing for the division between good and bad literature, narrative is international, transhistorical, transcultural: it is simply there, like life itself. (Barthes, 1977: 79)

Transnational, transhistorical, transcultural: indeed, even the interest in narratives dates from much earlier than the 1970s. The beginnings of narrative analysis can well be placed in the hermeneutic studies of the Bible, Talmud and Koran. Contemporary accounts usually begin with the work of a Russian formalist, Vladimir Propp, who published his *Morphology of the Folktale* in 1928, meticulously analyzing what he saw as the underlying structure of Russian folktales. Russian formalists and then postformalists such as Mikhail Bakhtin continued to develop narrative analysis, but it first received wider recognition in 1958 when Propp's book was translated into French and English. It has been the second English edition, that of 1968, which has met with great attention within and outside literary theory.

The contemporary literary study of narrative, claims Donald E. Polkinghorne (1987), has its origins in four national traditions: Russian formalism, US new criticism, French structuralism, and German hermeneutics. Going even further back in time, much of linguistic and narrative analysis can be traced to the disciples of two comparative linguists: the Pole, Jan Niecislaw Baudouin de Courtenay (1845–1929), and the Swiss, Ferdinand de Saussure (1857–1913).[1] The Soviet revolution put an end to the cooperation between the East and the West, but émigrés such as Roman Jakobson (linguist), Tzvetan Todorov (literary theorist), and Algirdas Greimas (semiologist) continued to develop the East European tradition in France, while Mikhail Bakhtin and others persevered in their efforts behind the Iron Curtain.

What all these movements had in common, and contrary to traditional hermeneutics, was their interest in texts as such, not in the authors' intentions or the circumstances of the texts' production. Such was the main tenet of the New Criticism, as represented by Northrop Frye and Robert Scholes, who looked not only for universal plots but also for the evolution of the narrative in history. The French narratologists, such as Tzvetan Todorov and Roland Barthes, were more under the influence of the structuralism of the anthropologist Claude Lévi-Strauss, who had earlier read Propp. Lévi-Strauss, along with the US linguist Naom Chomsky, looked for the invariable structure of the universal human mind. Another criticism (but also extension) of traditional hermeneutics came from Germany. Hans-Georg Gadamer (1900–2002) is best known as a promoter of contemporary hermeneutics. Wolfgang Iser and Hans Robert Jauss went further, creating their own reception theory; Iser especially puts emphasis on the interaction between the reader and the text (Iser, 1978). Among all those there was, and is, the formidable presence of Paul Ricoeur, who took into consideration those aspects of various schools that related to his main interest: the relation between temporality and narrative (Ricoeur, 1984; 1986).

This interest in narrative spread beyond literary theory to the humanities and social sciences. Historian Hayden White shocked by claiming that there can be no discipline of history, only of historiography, as historians emplot the events into histories instead of 'finding' them (White, 1973). William Labov and Joshua Waletzky espoused and improved on Propp's formalist analysis, suggesting that sociolinguistics should concern itself with a syntagmatic analysis of simple narratives, which would eventually provide a key to understanding the structure and function of complex narratives (Labov and Waletzky, 1967: 12–13). Richard Harvey Brown, in a peculiar act of parallel invention, spoke of 'a poetics for sociology' (1977), seemingly unaware that Mikhail Bakhtin had postulated it before him (Bakhtin, 1928/1985).

By the end of the 1970s, the trickle became a stream. Walter R. Fisher (1984) pointed out the central role of narrative in politics and of narrative analysis in political sciences; Jerome Bruner (1986) and Donald E. Polkinghorne (1987) did the same for psychology; Laurel Richardson (1990) for sociology; while Deirdre McCloskey (1990) scrutinized the narrative of economic expertise. By the 1990s, narrative analysis had also become a common approach in science studies (see, e.g., Curtis, 1994; Silvers, 1995).

Enacted narrative as a basic form of social life

One of the reasons for an eager espousal of a narrative approach in both the humanities and social sciences might be that it is useful to think of an enacted narrative as the most typical form of social life (MacIntyre, 1981/1990: 129). This need not be an ontological claim; life might or might not be an enacted narrative but conceiving of it as such provides a rich source of insight. This suggestion is at least as old as Shakespeare and has been taken up and elaborated upon by Kenneth Burke (1945), Clifford Geertz (1980), Victor Turner (1982), Ian Mangham and Michael Overington (1987), and many others.

Let me then begin with the basic tenet of Alasdair MacIntyre's philosophy: that social life is a narrative. It is usually assumed that social life consists of actions and events, where the difference between the two is as assumed intentionality of actions. In many social science texts, however, the term 'action' has been replaced by or used as an alternative for 'behavior'. In my own field, 'organizational behavior' is a term that is taken for granted – unproblematic even for otherwise critical authors and readers. But is there any reason to argue about the difference between 'action' and 'behavior'? There is, if we recall that the notion of 'behavioral sciences' goes back to eighteenth-century empiricism, in which the 'sense-datum' was proposed as the main unit of cognition and the main object of scientific study. Were we to describe our experience in terms of sensory description only, 'we would be confronted with not only an uninterpreted, but an uninterpretable world' (MacIntyre, 1981/1990: 79). Such a world would indeed be a world of 'behaviors', both meaningless and mechanical, because if sense-data were to become the basis for the formulation of laws, all reference to intentions, purposes, and reasons – all that which changes behavior into a human action – would have to be removed.[2]

MacIntyre and many other advocates of a narrative approach to social phenomena limit the concept of action to human beings: 'Human beings can be held to account for that of which they are the authors; other beings cannot' (MacIntyre, 1981/1990: 209). In Chapter 6 I show that such a limitation is not necessary but, at present, let us remain with the authors who were interested in grasping human conduct via the notion of narrative. Thus Alfred Schütz

(1899–1959) pointed out that it is impossible to understand human conduct while ignoring its intentions, and it is impossible to understand human intentions while ignoring the settings in which they make sense (Schütz, 1973). Such settings may be institutions, sets of practices, or some other contexts created by humans – contexts which have a history, within which both particular deeds and whole histories of individual actors can be and have to be situated in order to be intelligible.

The concept of action in the sense of an intentional act occurring between actors in a given social order (Harré, 1982) can be further related to three relevant traditions of thought. One is literary hermeneutics as represented by Ricoeur (1981), who suggested that meaningful action might be considered as a text, and vice versa. Meaningful action shares the constitutive features of the text; it becomes objectified by inscription, which frees it from its agent; it has relevance beyond its immediate context; and it can be read like an 'open work'. The *theory of literary interpretation* can thus be extended to the field of social sciences.

The second important tradition is that of *phenomenology*, introduced into the social sciences by Alfred Schütz and his pupils, Peter Berger and Thomas Luckmann. Phenomenology's encounter with US pragmatism produced two offshoots that are relevant to the present context. One is symbolic interactionism as represented by Herbert Blumer and Howard S. Becker. Another is ethnomethodology as developed by Harold Garfinkel, Aaron Cicourel, and Harvey Sacks. Their inspiration was taken up with particular success by the British sociologist, David Silverman (see, e.g., Silverman, 1975; Silverman and Jones, 1976; Silverman and Torode, 1980).

Ethnomethodology is significant here because it introduces the notion of accountability as a central concept in the understanding of social action. Accountability is the main bond of human interactions; indeed, the main social bond. Conduct can be treated as an action when it can be *accounted for* (before, simultaneously, or after the act – Harré, 1982) in terms that are acceptable in a given social setting. People spend their lives planning, commenting upon, and justifying what they and others do. Although some of this takes place in imaginary conversations conducted in people's heads, most takes place in 'real' conversations with others.

A limitation of traditional ethnomethodological thought is that it has difficulty in explaining the connections between different rules of accounting that appear to be ascribed to specific situations. A 'conversation between lovers' runs along a different script from a 'conversation of a teenager with her angry mother', but conversations between lovers and between teenagers and their angry mothers occurring in the same place over the same time period tend to resemble one another. How is this possible? Latour (1993b) suggested that ethnomethodology could explain *sociality, but not society*: there is nothing to fix various actions, to make situations repeatable. For him, technology is such a fixing and connecting device. In the example above, movies and TV have done a lot to propagate appropriate conversation scripts, for lovers and for teenagers. Speaking more generally, it is reproduction technologies that permit locating present conversations in history – that is, in past conversations.

Observing how conversations are repeated and how they change permits their classification into genres, as in literary criticism. One of the most central contemporary genres is that of life story: biography or autobiography. Although that which Elisabeth Bruss (1976) called 'autobiographical acts' existed as early as the seventeenth and eighteenth centuries, they were regarded as private documents. 'Biography' became a recognized term after 1680, but the term 'autobiography' was found in English texts only in 1809 (Bruss, 1976). It is therefore appropriate to pay attention to this genre of narrative, looking for a clue to understanding other modern genres. Its common characteristic is that a narrative of an individual history is placed in a narrative of social history (be it a family or a nation) or even in a history of the narrative.

As to the first narrative (that of an individual history), its importance is connected with the fact that in order to understand their own lives people put them into narrative form – and they do the same when they try to understand the lives of others. Thus actions acquire meaning by gaining a place in a narrative of life. 'Living is like writing a book' is a saying known in many languages.

This sounds as if people could tell stories as they please and, in so doing, shape their lives as they see fit. This is actually a typical criticism of social constructivism: that it conceives the world as a collection of subjectively spun stories.[3] But we are never the sole authors of our own narratives; in every conversation a *positioning* takes place (Davies and Harré, 1991) which is accepted, rejected, or improved upon by the partners in the conversation. When a new head of department introduces herself to her collaborators, she tells them how she wants to be perceived. Their reactions will tell her how much of this has been accepted or rejected, what corrections have been made, and how the members of the group want to be perceived by their new boss. But the end of the introductory meeting does not end the positioning thus begun; this will continue as long as these people work together, and even longer in the history they will tell later.

What is more, other people or institutions concoct narratives for others without including them in a conversation; *this is what power is about.* Some people decide about other people's jobs, their livelihoods, their identities. But even as puppets in a power game, people are still co-authors of history – that other enacted dramatic narrative in which they are also actors.

How can individual narratives be related to societal ones? To understand a society or some part of a society, it is important to discover its repertoire of legitimate stories and find out how it evolved – this is what I have called above a history of narratives. Thus, as MacIntyre reminds his readers, the chief means of moral education in pre-modern societies was the telling of stories in a genre fitting the kind of society whose story was being told. In the process of socialization or, as anthropologists call it, enculturation, young people were helped to attribute meaning to their lives by relating them to the legitimate narrative of the society to which they belonged. Thus the main narrative of, and in, heroic societies was epic and saga, whereas the genre of city-states was tragedy, both reflecting and expressing the prevalent stance toward human fate and human community.

Although neither of these cultures (the heroic societies nor the Greek city-states) was exactly unitary or consistent, MacIntyre nonetheless claims that it was only medieval cultures that first encountered the problem of multiple narratives on a global scale – with many ideals, many ways of life, many religions. How, then, could anybody tell a particular story? To begin with, it is obvious that every age hosts many competing narratives (indeed, periodization itself belongs to one story or another) and, in principle, one could choose to relate such a story to any of them. On the other hand, it makes sense for interpretive purposes to speak of a dominant or prevalent narrative genre at any one time – what is called in science the mainstream.

The novel, for instance, is regarded as the most characteristic genre of modern times. Kundera (1988) places Cervantes together with Descartes among the founders of the Modern Era. Other new genres emerged in modernity, such as the above-mentioned biography and autobiography (both a consequence of the modern institution of personal identity), while others changed their character so that a 'modern poetry' emerged, for instance. Thus when we read Giambattista Vico (1668–1744), the forerunner of modern ethnology, we know that we are reading a philosophical treatise and that it is not a modern one. In this sense genres are like any other institutions, or maybe all institutions are like genres: 'A literary institution must reflect and give focus to some consistent need and sense of possibility in the community it serves, but at the same time, a genre helps to define what is possible and to specify the appropriate means for meeting an expressive need' (Bruss, 1976: 5).

If we add instrumental needs to expressive needs (or better still if we remove any divide between them), social theory and social practice can be treated as special genres of narrative situated within other narratives of modern (or postmodern) society. Social sciences can therefore focus on how these narratives of theory and practice are constructed, used, and misused. But before moving on to concrete examples, we will examine the present understanding of the concept of narrative in social sciences and humanities. Two such perspectives are especially relevant: seeing narrative as a *mode of knowing* and narration as a *mode of communication*.

Narrative as a mode of knowing

Knowledge is not the same as science, especially in its contemporary form. (Lyotard, 1979/1986: 18)

In 1979, the Conseil des Universités of the government of Quebec asked French philosopher, Jean-François Lyotard, to write 'a report on knowledge in the most highly developed societies' (Lyotard, 1979/1986: xxv). In his report, Lyotard contrasted the narrative form of knowledge, typical of the non-modern type of society, with that modern invention – scientific knowledge. There is a peculiar relationship between the two, he said: while science requires narrative for its own legitimation (there has to be a story to tell why scientific knowledge is important at all), it repays the favor in poor coin.[4] Not only does it refuse to perform the same service and to legitimize narrative knowledge (with the possible exception of structuralism and formalism in literary theory) but also it fiercely denies narrative its legitimacy as a form of knowledge and, above all, demands that the question of knowledge status and legitimation remains taken for granted, unexamined. Paradoxically, however, as the grand narratives of legitimation lost their privileged status, narrative and science both came back into the light of scrutiny.

One of the authors to take up this scrutiny was Jerome Bruner, who compared the *narrative mode of knowing*[5] with the logico-scientific mode, also referred to as the paradigmatic mode of knowing (Bruner, 1986). The narrative mode of knowing consists in organizing experience with the help of a scheme assuming the intentionality of human action. Using the basic concepts of literary theory, Polkinghorne (1987) followed Bruner's lead in exploring the narrative, an attempt that I will discuss here at length in order to point out its interesting tenets.

Plot, says Polkinghorne, is the basic means by which specific events, otherwise represented as lists or chronicles, are brought into one meaningful whole. 'The company suffered unprecedented losses' and 'the top managers were forced to resign' are two mysterious events that call for interpretation. 'With the company suffering unprecedented losses, the top managers were forced to resign' is a narrative. The difference lies in the temporal ordering and thus in a suggested connection between the two. As the example indicates, some kind of causality may be inferred but it is crucial to see that narrative, unlike science, leaves *open* the nature of the connection. A law-type statement such as 'when a company suffers losses, its managers resign' invites falsification or verification on a statistical scale, but not a re-making and negotiation of meaning, such as: 'Are you sure? I've heard they started losing when the managers resigned, as they took their customers with them?'

What is considered a vice in science – openness to competing interpretations – is a virtue in narrative. This openness means that the same set of events can be organized around different plots. 'The top managers were forced to resign when it became clear that the company's losses were covered up for a long time' or 'The top managers were forced to resign even if the auditors were to blame' gives the same chain of events a different meaning. In 2002, the year of the Enron, World Com and Arthur Anderson scandals, such tentative plots were found daily in the media.

Polkinghorne also discusses a special type of *explanation* that is possible within a narrative, where the 'motives' can be reconciled with 'causes' in an interpretation of action. Within the logico-scientific mode of knowing, an explanation is achieved by recognizing an event as an instance of a general law, or as belonging to a certain category. Within the narrative mode of knowing, an explanation consists in relating an event to a human project:

> When a human event is said not to make sense, it is usually not because a person is unable to place it in the proper category. The difficulty stems, instead, from a person's inability to integrate the event into a plot whereby it becomes understandable in the context of what has happened ... Thus, narratives *exhibit* an explanation instead of demonstrating it. (Polkinghorne, 1987: 21)

Notice also the implicit differentiation between an 'event' and an 'action': the latter is an event that can be interpreted, made sense of, by attributing intentions to it. 'A flood' is an event but 'a flood due to the poor quality of cement used in the dam construction' is quite another story. While a logico-scientific text would have to demonstrate and prove the difference between the two, a narrative can simply put the elements close to one another, exhibiting an explanation: 'As water sprang in all directions, the engineer looked up and saw the growing hole in the dam.'

While it may be clear that narrative offers an alternative mode of knowing, the relative advantage of using this mode may remain obscure. Bruner (1990) points out that in narrative it is the plot rather than the truth or falsity of story elements that determines the power of the narrative as a story. A narrative which says 'The top managers resigned and then it rained a whole week' (i.e. a narrative with no plot or an incomprehensible plot) will need some additional elements to make sense of it, even though the two events and their temporal connection may well be true and correct in themselves. Bruner (1990: 44) calls this the narrative's *indifference to extralinguistic reality*, which is compensated by an extreme sensibility to the reality of the speech (i.e. the occasion when the narrative is presented). 'The top managers resigned, and then it rained the whole week' may produce an outburst of hilarity when, for example, told on a sunny day by the new CEO to his board of directors. There are no structural differences between fictional and factual narratives, and their respective attraction is not determined by their claim to be fact or fiction. The attractiveness of a narrative is situationally negotiated – or, rather, arrived at, since contingency plays as much a part in the process as esthetics or politics. This negotiation takes place even when readers are reading in solitude – a sleepy reader will find a text less attractive than an alert reader, etc.

Is there no way to tell the difference between a fictional and factual text, between *belles lettres* and social science, for that matter? There is, and to explain it I will borrow from Tzvetan Todorov, the Bulgarian-French literature theorist and linguist with a great interest in social sciences, his concept of a *fictional contract* (1978/1990: 26). In this tacit contract between the author and the reader, the authors plead: suspend your disbelief, as I am going to please you. In what can be called a *referential contract*, the researcher pleads: activate your disbelief, as I am going to instruct you. It goes without saying that if the scientific author manages to please the reader as well, it is a bonus.

In the meantime, the lack of structural differences between fictional and factual narratives is suspected to account for most of their power. Narrative thrives on the contrast between the ordinary, what is 'normal', usual, and expected, and the 'abnormal', unusual, and unexpected. It has effective means at its disposal for rendering the unexpected intelligible: 'The function of the story is to find an intentional state that mitigates or at least makes comprehensible a deviation from a canonical cultural pattern' (Bruner, 1990: 49–50). This is possible because the power of the story does not depend on its connection to the world outside the story but in its openness for negotiating meaning. 'This is a true story' and 'This never happened' are two ways of claiming genre affiliation, but genre affiliation does not decide whether a story is found interesting or not. *Se non è vero è ben trovato* (even if it's untrue it is still beautifully put), says an Italian proverb.

As narratives explaining deviations are socially sensitive, a form of story whose power does not reside in the difference between fact and fiction is convenient for such sensitive negotiations. One or many alternative narratives are always in the offing. In Enron's story, the blame and, consequently, the part of the Villain, was given in alternative versions to the US government, to Enron's executives, to auditors, or to all of them. The events acquire a meaning by the application of *abduction* (a guess, a tentative plot), which introduces a hypothetical connection – just like a hypothesis but still claiming openness. Yet another story might offer a better or more convincing explanation, without ever challenging the truth or falsity of the story elements. There is no way of deciding between different stories except by negotiation: between the writers (as in a public debate), between the writer and the reader (where the writer tries to get the upper hand but the reader has the last word), or between various readers, as in a private conversation. Stories, claims Bruner, are 'especially viable instruments for social negotiation'.

This 'method of negotiating and renegotiating meanings by the mediation of narrative interpretation', it seems to Bruner, 'is one the crowning achievements of human development in the ontogenetic, cultural and phylogenetic sense of that expression' (1990: 67). The human species developed a 'protolinguistic' readiness for the narrative organization of experience. This primitive disposition of the child is encouraged and elaborated in the course of life, exploiting the richness of the existing repertoire of stories and plots. An adult person will enrich, challenge, and continue this repertoire.

The analogy between the enculturation of a child and an acculturation of an immigrant or a new employee is obvious, but I want to carry the point even further. Even scientists become scientists with the help of narrative. Graduate students read mountains of books on methods, like this one, but when they want to submit their first paper to a referee journal, they ask a colleague who has already published: 'How did you go about it?' The method books are accompanied by growing numbers of biographies and autobiographies, and they themselves are richly illustrated with stories.

It is not difficult to admit that narrative knowledge is ubiquitous in all social practices. Managers and their subordinates tell stories and write stories, to one another and to interviewers, be they researchers or journalists. So do doctors and patients, teachers and pupils, salespersons and customers, coaches and foot-ball players. The genre of autobiography – personal and organizational – is steadily growing in popularity, while the older types of stories – folktales, myths, and sagas – acquire new forms thanks to new technologies and new media.

A student of social practices re-tells narratives of a given practice and con-structs them herself, first and second hand. Nevertheless, she cannot stop here as, by doing that, she will be barely competing with the practitioners them-selves, and from a disadvantaged position. She must go further and see how the narratives of practice unfold. This interest can lead her to a stance espousing the ideas of logico-scientific knowledge, as formalism and structuralism tended to do, or those closer to the poststructuralist edge of the spectrum of narratol-ogy. I shall introduce both types but, before that, we will look at another use of narrative – narration as a communication mode.

Narration as a mode of communication

Narration is a common mode of communication. People tell stories to enter-tain, to teach and to learn, to ask for an interpretation and to give one. When US political scientist, Walter Fisher, read MacIntyre's work, he suddenly under-stood that his own work in the area of communication had stemmed from a conception of the human being as *Homo narrans* (Fisher, 1984). From this emerged an attempt to combine the narrative and paradigmatic modes of know-ing in what he calls a *narrative paradigm* of communication.

The narrative paradigm is based on a notion of *narrative rationality* (Fisher, 1987), in contrast to the conventional model of formal rationality whereby human communication is supposed to follow the rules of formal logic.[6] Rationality as redefined by Fisher involves the principles of *narrative probability* – a story's coherence and integrity – and *narrative fidelity* – a story's credibility established by the presence of 'good reasons' (i.e. 'accurate assertions about social reality') (Fisher, 1987). This redefinition of rationality, he claims, provides a radical democratic ground for a social-political critique, inasmuch as it assumes that everybody is capable of narrative rationality. Unlike the traditional notion of rationality, it also allows for interpretation of public moral argument (see also R.H. Brown, 1998). Fisher demonstrated the use of his concepts in his analysis of the nuclear war controversy as a public moral argument (1984) and of the political rhetoric of Ronald Reagan (1987).

Fisher's claim that 'all forms of human communication need to be seen fundamentally as stories' (1987: xiii) can be regarded as both narrower and more extensive than MacIntyre's conception of narrative. According to my reading of the latter, narrative is the main form of social life because it is the main device for making sense of social action. Thus it either subsumes communication as a kind of action or makes it redundant (everything is 'communication'). However, if one insists on preserving the notion of communication to denote a special kind of social action, it becomes clear that there are other forms of human communication than narrative. Fisher has himself enumerated several: technical argument, poetic discourse, or such speech acts Gumbrecht (1992) called description and argumentation.

Some discourses or speech acts may aim at the destruction or at least the interruption of the narrative. The Dada movement in art provides an extreme example of an experiment in human communication which opposed the storytelling mode and yet we make sense of it by placing it in the narrative of Modern Art or, alternatively, in the narrative of European history at the moment when post-World War I frustration was at its height (Berman, 1992).

Fisher also wants to conduct a 'criterial analysis' of narratives: it is not enough for him to see narrative as good or bad *for the purpose at hand*, to paraphrase Schütz. Consequently, he rejects pragmatism while sharing many of its ideas. His understanding of rationality is still geared to the *application of criteria* rather than the *achievement of consensus* (Rorty, 1992). This means that, while espousing the narrative mode of knowing, Fisher does not want to abandon the paradigmatic (logico-scientific) one; hence his expression 'the narrative paradigm'. There must be a priori criteria for what is good or bad in telling stories. This requirement recalls the argument in Habermas (1984) that there must be a set of criteria for a good dialogue external to the dialogue itself. Fisher does, in fact, acknowledge his debt to the German philosopher.

I am dwelling on this issue to warn the readers that I adopt a new pragmatist view. Consequently, while sympathizing with many of Fisher's ideas, I do not espouse his overall purpose: 'It is a corollary of the general pragmatist claim that there is no permanent ahistorical metaphysical framework into which everything can be fitted' (Rorty, 1992: 64). I do not accuse Fisher of planning to come up with such a framework but his criteria certainly look as though they could be fitted into one. Pragmatically again, it is possible to envisage many situations in which the construction of such criteria might well serve a particular purpose. Once they have received a special status, however, they will end up as 'principles' and 'criteria' usually do: obstructing their own change or reform.

The notion of an 'ideal speech situation', coined by Habermas (1984), achieved wide resonance in organization theory and practice, especially as a way of improving organizational communication (Gustavsen, 1985). A similar success can be predicted for Fisher's ideas, which lend themselves well to consultancy purposes: with a list of 'conditions for a good narrative', organizational communication can surely be improved. And yet understanding of organizational reality, such as informs the present book, indicates that such an effort is impossible. 'An ideal speech situation' and 'a good narrative' are things that have to be locally negotiated, and those are valid only for a given time and place. They are results not preconditions of organizational communication. Some claim that this phenomenon of the constant construction of society is in itself local and temporal and belongs to 'late modernity' or 'postmodernity'.

Is there room for narrative in a postmodern society?

While there is general agreement that the epoch in which we now live is different from that which is called 'modernity' (although it is not yet sure how, as epochs are best named after they ended), there is disagreement about the type of reflection that has been called 'postmodern'. For some, 'postmodern' is merely a description of a school of architecture and any other use of the word is unwarranted. For others, 'postmodern' means a pretentious, hermetic vocabulary, plaguing mostly the humanities, but recently also the social sciences. In this text, 'postmodern' is applied to a kind of social reflection that is characterized by three tenets:

1   It refuses the correspondence theory of truth, according to which statements are true where they correspond to the world, on the basis that it is impossible to compare words to non-words (Rorty, 1980).
2   Consequently, it challenges the operation of representation, revealing the complications of any attempt to represent something by something else.
3   And, therefore, it pays much attention to language (in a sense of any system of signs – numbers, words, or pictures) as a tool of reality construction rather than its passive mirroring.

It might seem, however, that this text goes against the grain of what is one of the main tenets in the postmodern reflection – that is, that 'history has come to an end' (Fukuyama, 1992) or that the grand narratives – of progress, of emancipation, and recently even of economic growth – have been abandoned (Lyotard, 1979). Answering Lyotard on behalf of the pragmatists, Rorty claims that 'we want to drop *meta*narratives, but keep on recounting edifying first-order narratives' (1992: 60). History may be dead but only if we were attached irrevocably to one specific version of it. Abandoning the modern metanarrative of emancipation does not mean giving up the longing for narratives that we happen to like in a benign ethnocentrism which values our own way of life but relinquishes the idea of 'modernizing' other people who are 'underdeveloped', 'premodern', or in some other way different from us. A quest for a good life extends to becoming a quest for a good society, excluding a missionary zeal which forces other people to adopt our point of view but including a readiness to listen to other people and their narratives so that we might include them in our own narrative if we happen to like them (Rorty, 1991). And Lyotard agrees: it was only the narratives of legitimation, the 'metanarratives,' which were exposed to the postmodern critique: 'the little narrative remains the quintessential form of imaginative invention, most particularly in science' (1979/1986: 61).

The question then arises as to whether it is in fact possible to construct any shared concepts, whether it is possible to have a conversation, an exchange of narratives – without recourse to a metanarrative of some kind. In answering this, MacIntyre (1981/1990) emphasizes the unpredictability of an enacted dramatic narrative of life and history. Such construction is never finished and in the negotiation of meaning the results are for ever uncertain. The old metanarratives sinned in their ambition to end a conversation by trying to predict its outcome. If a canon is already known, there is nothing left to talk about.

The narrative structure of human life requires unpredictability and this is, paradoxically, why the alleged failure of the social sciences (namely, their failure to formulate laws and consequently the failure to predict) is in fact their greatest achievement. According to MacIntyre, this should be interpreted not as a defeat but as a triumph, as virtue rather than vice. He adds provocatively that the common claim that the human sciences are young in comparison with the natural sciences is clearly false, and they are in fact as old, if not older. And the kind of explanations they offer fit perfectly the kind of phenomena they purport to explain.

Unpredictability[7] does not imply inexplicability. Explanations are possible because there is a certain teleology – sense of purpose – in all lived narratives. It is a kind of circular teleology because it is not given beforehand but is created by the narrative. A life is lived with a goal but the most important aspect of life is the formulation and re-formulation of that goal. This circular teleology is what MacIntyre calls a *narrative quest*. A virtuous life, according to him, is a life dedicated to a quest for the good human life, where the construction of a definition of a 'good life' is a process that ends only when a life comes to an end. Rather than being defined at the outset, a 'good life' acquires a performative definition through the living of it. A search looks for something that already exists (as in a 'search for excellence'); a quest creates its goal rather than discovers it. The proponents of means–ends rationality defend the notion of the a priori goals, while the pragmatists declare it to be impractical. A narrative view gets rid of the problem by reinstating the role of goals as both the results and the antecedents of action. Whole communities as well as individual persons are engaged in a quest for meaning in 'their life', which will bestow meaning on particular actions taken.

Therefore a student of social life, no matter of which domain, needs to become interested in narrative as a form of social life, a form of knowledge, and a form of communication.

There is an apparent difference between MacIntyre and Fisher, on the one hand, and another advocate of a narrative approach, Richard Harvey Brown, on the other, as regards the role of narrative in contemporary society. The first two celebrate narratives whereas Brown sees them as an endangered species: 'Narrative requires a political economy and collective psychology in which a sense of lived connection between personal character and public conduct prevails' (1987: 144). This condition, Brown claims, is rare in contemporary western societies, where personal character has become separated from public conduct (see also Sennett, 1998). The difference is misleading in that both MacIntyre and Fisher feel there is a need to celebrate narrative precisely *because* there is a rift between private and public discourse, *because* the language of virtues has become obsolete (MacIntyre, 1981/1990), and *because* a public moral argument has become an oxymoron in the light of emotive ethics (Fisher, 1984; 1987). All three authors – and indeed most of the adherents of the narrative mode of knowing, whether or not they call themselves such – are vitally interested in constructing a public moral discourse which avoids nostalgia trips to the past (especially to totalitarian pasts) and does not stop at denouncing the postmodern fragmentation. They may differ in their view on the ultimate purpose (emancipation for Fisher and Brown, a quest for virtues for MacIntyre, and a fight against cruelty for Rorty), but there is always a moral vision in their theories.[8]

About this book

Figure 1.1 depicts various uses of narrative and its analysis in social science studies, simultaneously announcing the contents of this book. Thus Chapter 2 concerns the ways in which stories are made in various fields of practice (including scientific practice, although this field receives more attention in Chapters 8 and 9). Chapter 3 concerns story collection, while Chapter 4 shows that interviews allow all three activities, being an observation of how stories are made, an opportunity for story collection, and a possibility to provoke storytelling. Chapter 5 introduces a general framework of text interpretation. Chapter 6 illustrates structuralist ways of analyzing texts, whereas Chapter 7 introduces poststructuralist and deconstructivist ways of reading a text. Chapter 8 offers examples of readings of scientific texts, while Chapter 9 discusses issues important in writing a scientific text. Chapter 10 discusses the consequences of narrativizing social sciences.

Chapters 2–9 have a similar structure: they begin with a general introduction of a given aspect of a narrative approach, continue with one or more examples of well-known works illustrating this very aspect, and end with a detailed example of a given textual operation. Examples are often taken from my own work, not because it is exemplary but because it permits me to take liberties impossible to take with texts of other authors. Chapters 1–9 end with one or more 'exercises' whose aim is to create material that can be used in exemplifying the contents of the next chapter. The readers can replace the exercise material with their own field

Field of practice

- Watch how the stories are being made
  - Collect the stories
    - Provoke story telling
      - Interpret the stories (what do they say?)
        - Analyze the stories (how do they say it?)
          - Deconstruct the stories (unmake them)
            - Put together your own story
              - Set it against/together with other stories

Field of research

material. Chapter 10 does not contain an exercise as the exercise is the reader's own text – to be created. All chapters end with a 'further reading list' that might serve as a guide among the long list of references to a reader who wants to deepen his or her introduction to the narrative approach to social sciences.

EXERCISE

Exercise 1.1: my life so far

Write a chronological account of your own life. (If you are working in a group, decide from the start whether you want to share your biography with the others. A conscious censorship works better than a subconscious one.)

FURTHER READING

Bruner, Jerome (1986) *Actual Minds, Possible Worlds.* Cambridge, MA: Harvard University Press.
Czarniawska, Barbara (1997) *Narrating the Organization. Dramas of Institutional Identity.* Thousand Oaks, CA: Sage.
Fisher, Walter R. (1987) *Human Communication as Narration: Toward a Philosophy of Reason, Value and Action.* Columbia, SC: University of South Carolina Press.
Nash, Christopher (ed.) (1990) *Narrative in Culture: The Uses of Storytelling in the Sciences, Philosophy and Literature.* London: Routledge.
Mitchell, W.J.T. (ed.) (1980) *On Narrative.* Chicago, IL: University of Chicago Press.
Polkinghorne, Donald E. (1987) *Narrative Knowing and the Human Sciences.* New York, NY: SUNY Press.

Notes

1   For a short description of their work see, e.g., *The New Encyclopædia Britannica* (1990): Micropædia, Vol. 1: 969; Vol. 10: 427.
2   This feat was, of course, never accomplished, although seriously attempted. The best example of lingering ambiguity is the famous – and infamous – psychological notion of 'attitude' which, by insisting on preserving the mechanical together with the intentional, promised much and gave little.
3   For a review of criticisms against social constructionism, and a defense, see Czarniawska (2003a).
4   Richard Harvey Brown (1998) shows how Descartes and Copernicus created acceptance for their scientific apparatuses by placing them in 'narratives of conversion'.
5   An interesting tautology, as Bruner points out: 'narrative' in Latin probably comes from *gnarus* ('knowing').
6   Here once again one is reminded of the ethnomethodological redefinition of rationality as a rhetoric to account for social actions (Garfinkel, 1967).
7   Unpredictability is far from total: there are predictabilities that we ourselves create (as in timetables); there is predictability in statistical regularities; there is knowledge of causal regularities in nature and social life.
8   This should not be taken as moralizing; the authors' interests mentioned here lie in improving the discourse on morality not in telling people or nations what they should do with their lives.

2

How Stories are Made

This chapter introduces a differentiation between narratives as purely chronological accounts and stories as emplotted narratives. Consequently, it focuses on work of ordering – seen as collective efforts at emplotment in everyday life and work.

Narratives into stories

The quotation from Barthes that opened Chapter 1 represents the most inclusive definition of narrative encountered in texts on narrative analysis: everything is a narrative or at least can be treated as one. Usually, however, a narrative is understood as a spoken or written text giving an account of an event/action or series of events/actions, chronologically connected. Indeed, it is easy to say what is not a narrative even if it is a text: a table, a list, a schedule, a typology (Goody, 1986).

Historian Hayden White, in *The Content of the Form* (1987), has convincingly demonstrated the advantages of a narrower definition of narrative, indeed of distinguishing between a narrative and a story. He described how the way of writing history in Europe changed with time. *Annals* registered only some dates and events and did not attempt to connect them. *Chronicles* presented some causal connections but were devoid of plot or a meaningful structure. Only the products of the modern way of writing history can earn recognition as stories that are more than chronological compilations. White quotes the example of the 'Annals of Saint Gall' as most typical of early European historiography:

709. Hard winter. Duke Gottfried died.
710. Hard winter and deficient in crops.
711.
712. Flood everywhere.
713.
714. Pippin, mayor of the palace, died.
715. 716. 717.
718. Charles devastated the Saxons with great destruction.
719.
720. Charles fought against the Saxons.
721. Theudo drove the Saracens out of Aquitaine.
722. Great crops.
723.
724.
725. Saracens came for the first time.
726. 727. 728. 729. 730.
731. Blessed Bede, the presbyter, died.
732. Charles fought against the Saracens at Poitiers on Saturday.
733.
734. (White, 1987: 16)

A *History of France by Richerus of Rheims* (c. 998) is, for White, an example of a chronicle – a narrative but not yet a (hi)story. It has a subject, a geographical location, a social center, and a beginning in time:

> But the work fails as proper history, at least according to the opinion of later commentators, by virtue of two considerations. First, the order of the discourse follows the order of chronology; it presents events in the order of their occurrence and cannot, therefore, offer the kind of meaning that a narratologically governed account can be said to provide. Second, probably owing to the 'annalistic' order of discourse, the account does not so much conclude as simply terminate; it merely breaks off … and throws onto the reader the burden of retrospectively reflecting on the linkages between the beginning of the account and its ending. (White, 1987: 17)

Thus, if the monks of Saint Gall decide to turn their annals into a chronicle, it could have looked like this (I am now taking liberties with White's and the monks' texts):

The year 709 was the beginning of harsh times for the land all around us. Two hard winters inevitably led to bad crops, and people were dying like flies. Among them was Duke Gottfried, mourned by all his people. And while it seemed that nature became benevolent again, flood struck in 712.

After that, however, God took mercy on his people. For a good five years nothing much happened, apart from the fact that Pippin, mayor of the palace, died. The great leader, Charles, successfully combated the Saxons in 718 and in 720, while his ally, Theudo, drove the Saracens out of Aquitaine. Crops were great in 722, and the land enjoyed peace when, in 725, the Saracens came for the first time. They were defeated but came again in 732, and reached as far as Poitiers. This happened almost immediately after Blessed Bede, our presbyter, died.

This is a narrative but it is still not a story as it lacks a plot. It needs to be emplotted. How can this be done? First, we need a working definition of a *plot*.

Todorov proposes such a definition of a minimal plot:

> [it] consists in the passage from one equilibrium to another. An 'ideal' narrative begins with a stable situation which is disturbed by some power or force. There results a state of disequilibrium; by the action of a force directed in the opposite direction, the equilibrium is re-established; the second equilibrium is similar to the first, but the two are never identical. (1971/1977: 111)

The second equilibrium may only resemble the first in that it is an equilibrium; it is not uncommon that its contents are the reverse of the first. A company in trouble may reorganize and become profitable again or it may go into bankruptcy, thus restoring market equilibrium. The episode that describes the passage from one state to another can have one or many elements: there can be one single force that changes the state of affairs into another one ('a paradigm shift') or a force and a counterforce; the two latter often consist of an event and an action (a flood and emergency management). Usually, plots are much more complicated and contain chains of actions and events, oscillating states of affairs, apparent actions, and wrongly interpreted events, as in *suspense* or *mystery*, but a minimal plot is enough to make sense of a narrative. Thus the famous excerpt used by Harvey Sacks (1992: 223–6) as material for two lectures ('The baby cried. The mommy picked it up') needs to be completed by a third sentence (e.g. 'The baby stopped crying') to become a story.

I will take a further liberty with White's and the *Annals'* text to try to complete the 'chronicle of St. Gall' into a proper story. Such stories, or histories, can be numerous, depending on who writes them. A contemporary historian, careful not to jump to conclusions, might thus turn the 'chronicle' above into a 'history' by adding a simple ending:

ENDING 1. As we can see, the early history of Europe was a constant fight against hostile nature and hostile invaders. [*Plot becomes circular; the second equilibrium never lasts, as either nature or invaders hit back.*]

A monk of Saint Gall, after having taken a course in narrative writing, would be more likely to pen something as follows (the added information about the Mass is speculation based on the fact that the battle was fought on Saturday):

ENDING 2. As we can see, the early history of France was the history of a people tried severely by their God who, however, was their only solace. When Blessed Bede died, Charles found it very difficult to lead his soldiers against the Saracens. But a great Mass was said on Sunday, after the victory. [*Christianity is the force of change and the way of accepting adversities.*]

Finally, a theoretician of leadership could emplot it still differently:

ENDING 3. As we can see, the presence of a strong leader was crucial for the survival of the people. When Duke Gottfried died, a harsh winter, deficient crops, and floods were felt painfully. When Charles took his place before his people, the hardship of nature ceased to occupy the minds of the people who bravely fought at the side of their leader. [*Leadership is the crucial factor between failure and success.*]

Although adding one paragraph at the end of a chronicle, as I have just done, is not the most sophisticated manner of plotting, it is not unusual. The end explains (one could say, retro-jects) logical connections between various episodes (for more on end-embedded plots, see Chapter 6). Usually, however, the work of plotting is more complex.

The ways of emplotment

Hayden White (1973) pointed out that, surprisingly enough, modern stories are often emplotted with the help of classical rhetorical tropes (figures of speech). There are four classical rhetorical figures or master tropes: metaphor, metonymy, synecdoche, and irony.

Tropes are figurative expressions. The word comes from *tropos* (Greek for 'turn') and is used to mark various 'turns' of a purely literal expression. *Metaphor*, perhaps the most well-known trope, explains a less known term by connecting it to one better known: 'the moon is a silver plate.' *Metonymy* substitutes something in the vicinity for the original object or its attribute for the object itself: the crown for the kingdom, the banner for the country. *Synecdoche* builds on the part–whole relationship where the part symbolizes the whole or the whole symbolizes the part: hands for workers, brains for intellectuals. *Irony* builds on inverted meaning – the opposite of what is ostensibly expressed. In *Pride and Prejudice*, Mr. Bennet, who is very fond of irony, says: 'I admire all my three sons-in-law-highly. Wickham, perhaps, is my favorite' (Lanham, 1991: 92).[1]

Tropes are not mere ornaments used to embellish speech or to deceive its audience. They permeate all linguistic utterances. They have affinities to certain dramaturgical conventions (that is, enacted and emplotted narratives), which are easily recognizable by an audience familiar with those conventions – in this case, an audience of European origins.

Romance is a narrative form focused on a single Character and his or her potentialities. Its standard plot is that of the knight's quest, the chivalry tale in which the hero, after a prolonged search including various trials and adventures, regains what is lost – love, the meaning of life, success and glory, or all the above. Metaphor is the basic rhetorical figure of Romance: the hero or the heroine symbolize order, their enemies represent the forces of Evil, etc. Romance is built on the romantic assumption that all creatures and things in the world have a true and deep meaning which, after purging his or her soul, the hero or the heroine can reveal and so an initial metaphor will in the end become a proper name.

Tragedy views humankind as subjected to a number of laws of fate, laid bare through the central crises that constitute the hub of the narration. Tragedy is built around metonymy as this classical rhetorical figure compares phenomena from a perspective of juxtaposition: phenomena or objects that are near to one another in time or space. A typical example is the tragic Sisyphus mythos, where the boulder, eternally pushed up the hill by the tragic hero and eternally rolling down again, stands for the fate of Sisyphus.

In *Comedy* human beings are not represented as subject to laws of fate but rather as organically forming parts of a higher unity which, despite setbacks and (funny) complications, works to resolve everything into harmony – the characteristic happy ending. Thus Comedy always moves between two societies, one deficient, the other desirable. In Comedy, the final state is a society that optimally integrates the Characters. The transition to the new and better society does not take place without friction; on the contrary, complications connected to it give fuel to the narration. A central role in these complications is played by 'obstructing characters' who are the comics of Comedy. On the other hand, there are always characters who support a happy ending. Both these types of characters are functionally or dysfunctionally linked to the harmonious working of the whole society. This is why the rhetorical figure corresponding to Comedy is synecdoche, the trope that represents the whole by one of its parts.

Satire shows the absurdity of all that occurs and therefore also of all the previously mentioned narrative conventions. It must reject as illusions the rational laws of fate in Tragedy, the pursuit of a common harmony in Comedy, and the self-fulfillment and disclosure of true meaning in Romance. Irony – the trope of skepticism, of contradiction, and of paradox – is the favored rhetorical figure of Satire.[2]

The Swedish organization scholar, Kaj Sköldberg, discovered that different representations of organizational change he was studying were emplotted using these classical plots, thus resulting in different versions of the same sequence of events (Sköldberg, 1994; 2002). One version of the change was tragic. The organization has ended up in a crisis due to a fatal error: it has suffered from ignorance of the inexorable laws of fate – in this case a lack of cost awareness, the symptom of which is serious hubris concerning expenses and the prospects of expansion. The problem was being solved by means of rationalization. These may be saving measures; the drama can then be played in the genre of triumphant Tragedy. The means may also be computerization, which belongs to another tragic genre, the fatalistic one: computers are usually represented as *deus ex machina*, something one 'must' have because then all problems will be resolved.

Another version of the reorganization was a Romantic Comedy, performed for an enthusiastic audience. In theater as in life, romantic comedy is an all-time favorite. After all, Comedy always presents the transition from an original and deficient state of affairs to a final and desirable one. The initial state of the organizations Sköldberg studied was characterized by ridiculous regulations. The final state was deregulation, implicitly tied to a mythical Golden Age (i.e. free market before regulation). Deregulation meant an unhappy organization had to be divided into happy local subcommunities – hence decentralization. The main drama of Comedy was combined with diverse Romantic activities directed at the personnel (comically called 'human resource management'), through which the members of the organizations were expected to regain their true but forgotten selves.

In the third version, that of the critics of the reform, a tale was enacted according to the Satirical convention. It caricatured both the previous dramas, showing that they were incompatible. In addition, a general disintegration or decoupling appeared between the components of the change so that the genre could be defined as fragmented Satire. The decoupling varied in strength but was omnipresent in numerous variations: as a decoupling between decentralization and computerization, between problems and solutions, between power and power base, between management and employees, and between various symbols.

Sköldberg's exercise was not an eccentric application of classical genres to a contemporary material. Classical plots are easily recognizable and much appreciated by modern audiences. Although the same public appreciates and enjoys the revolutionary and experimental approaches of modern and postmodern drama, its tastes (in art and beyond) are often conservative. This is why it is so difficult to replace the traditional story of leadership as male pursuit by its feminine versions (see Chapter 7), or for that matter the Hollywood plot, where all ends in a happy ending. The classical repertoire of plots is very resilient.

Watching while stories are made

All the examples above indicate that sensemaking is a retrospective process, requiring time, but they do not actually demonstrate *how* a collective narrative is woven from disparate events. This is difficult to demonstrate because of the inevitable conflict between 'the prospective orientation of life with the retrospective orientation of narrative' (Ryan, 1993: 138). It is impossible to monitor the actors in order to capture the moments during which they elaborate their life experience into a story, not only in the case of the monks of St. Gall but even in the case of living actors. Yet Marie-Laure Ryan (1993) succeeded in locating what she calls 'a factory of plot' (p. 150): live radio broadcasts of sports events. There, 'the real life situation promotes a narrative tempo in which the delay between the time of occurrence of the narrated events and the time of their verbal representation strives toward zero, and the duration of the narration approximates the duration of the narrated' (p. 138). Thus, live broadcasts (not only of sports events) are of great interest to a narratively minded researcher.

A broadcast is constructed around three dimensions: *the chronicle* (what is happening), *the mimesis* (how does it look, a dimension that allows the listener to construct a virtual picture of the events), and the *emplotment* (how things are connected; a structure that makes sense of the events).

While emplotment is considered central for building a story, it is obviously the chronicle that is central to a sports broadcast. The necessity of matching the narrative time to real time creates specific challenges and responses. One is 'empty time' (the 'missing years' in the annals) when 'nothing' is happening on the field and the broadcasters fill it with past stories and general chat, at the risk of being caught in the middle of the story by a new event. Another is the congestion of events, a problem usually solved by quickening the pace of speech, sometimes to an impossible speed.

One way of filling empty time is to turn it to the service of the mimetic dimension of the broadcast. When there is a lull after a dramatic event, this event can be retold with an emphasis on how it happened.

The real challenge, however, is the emplotment of the broadcast. The broadcasters, says Ryan, perform it using three basic operations: *constructing characters* – that is, introducing legible differences between the actors (a hero and an opponent); *attributing a function* to single events; and *finding an interpretive theme* that subsumes the events and links them in a meaningful sequence ('near success', 'near failure', etc.: p. 141).

The close analogy between sports events and organizational performance in contemporary societies has been commented upon extensively (Corvellec, 1997; see also Chapter 8). Indeed, the spectators (e.g., the shareholders) insist on seeing the chronicle of the events, not least because they want to have an opportunity to make their own emplotment. Although the real interest concerns the plot ('why do you have losses?'), the loosely espoused principles of logico-scientific knowledge turn the attention away from the operation of emplotment. Plots are given (in the form of scientific laws) so the only activity required is to recognize their pattern in the chronicle. This hiding of the emplotment process results in the scarce interest in mimesis – on the part of the actors, spectators, and observers/researchers alike. And yet it is the mimesis, the how, that offers most rewards as to the way events become connected with the help of an accessible repertoire of plots: a dirty princess cannot marry a prince, a dishonest company cannot remain on a stock market, etc.

What prompted me to apply White's recipe for a chronicle and a history to the text of the annals was the analogy I saw between these three forms and the story making that I was able to watch during my study of management in three European capitals (Czarniawska, 2002). The minutes of my direct observation resembled annals, even if contemporary metrology permits a more detailed measure of time. Also, most organizational reports resemble annals (Gabriel, 2000). On the other hand, interview transcripts resembled chronicles: they reported the chronological and causal chains of events but did not have a point or a plot. After some time, however, I could see how complete stories begin to emerge. In certain situations, though, stories had to be produced at once.

During my study of city management in Warsaw I have been shadowing the director of the Metro Construction General Headquarters – a city-owned company that was building a subway in Warsaw which was hoping to operate it after it was built. Here are some excerpts from my observation:

Day 1.

14.00. I am sitting in Director General's (*D*) office talking to the Finance Director (*FD*).

FD: On Wednesday at 10 a.m. there will be a press conference with a participation of the City Mayor. One of the things discussed will be the metro ... You see, our organization dates from the times when contractors would choose an investor and the General Headquarters had the function of a super-contractor. Nowadays it is the investor that chooses contractors. For us, it would be the most advantageous to have one investor, and many contractors, where MCGH would have the role of the coordinator.

BC: What would be, according to you, an ideal organization structure for the Metro?

FD: I'm not a copyist and I don't believe that it's necessary to imitate something, but for me the Swiss are the model of democracy and good management. When it comes to the public transportation, they've solved it in the most reasonable way. Outside of Zurich, in cantons and municipalities...

14:50. Enters *D*.

> ...there are non-profit joint-stock companies, because metro is an unremunerative institution. Larger share means more money you put in, I believe such a solution would be the best one.

BC: Who are shareholders?

FD: Municipalities, districts. The Swiss solution admits persons who are interested in the development of the public transportation, but their participation is minimal, few percents and the rest belongs to a municipality in proportion to the quantity of transports. Depending on the management system you obtain specific results – the better financial arrangement the higher benefits, you have to pay less. Every administrative and economic decision is taken by voting, as every decision-maker has well-defined competencies. It's the democratic system that has been formed in 600 years and everybody cooperates together in an ideal symbiosis.

This is a draft of the first story, launched by FD: an ideal property structure for the future metro company, legitimated by the long history of Switzerland's success. 'Switzerland' serves as a Utopia: a land where everything works as it should:

FD: turns to *D*: You are invited to a press conference.

D: I won't be here – I have an appointment with a doctor. What it will be all about?

FD: Mainly about the investors and the contractors.

D: That's too bad. But what is to be the theme of the press conference?

FD: A great improvisation, as usual...

D: Did we make for the Deputy Mayor a list of the things we are doing?

FD: Yes, but I don't have it on me. I gave him 3 copies.

D: I understand that Mr. City Mayor will talk...

FD: And we will be sitting in the back... But at least his attitude was extremely peaceful.

D: All of them have changed, now they are all very nice. It was confirmed that the Council can't appoint or revoke contractors till the elections... but if the president and the parliament agree that the elections should be postponed for a year we will have to do something about it. All who were able to, have already settled their affairs and will sit and twiddle their thumbs ... We have to meet Mr. X from the county governor – to find out how the metro will be placed in the future governance system, whether it will be included in the City or in the county...

3:15 p.m. Enters the secretary.

S: Kislewski is on the phone.

D: The one that did the movies?

S: Not Kieslowski[3] but Kislewski. (*Turning* to FD): A Swiss company is
        calling to say that they guarantee completion of the tunnel.
FD: Tell them to call in three years.
S: Does it mean that we are not interested?
FD: We are, but in three years. The tunnels we did have been completed,
        and the next ones will be ready to be built in three years.
BC: Don't they know it?
FD: Probably not. But seriously, the construction of the next section of
        the metro will be feasible in three years... But we have the contrac-
        tors for the whole thing. Should I fire our miners?

10 minutes are spent in getting rid of Kislewski (*D* to *BC*: You know, here
everybody has to talk with the director).

The Director suggests that there is a more important interpretative theme than
the ideal shape of a company: the political positioning of the future metro
company. The real Swiss intervene. Observe my own story making: I am omitting parts of the conversation (...) and yet I keep the fragment about
Kislewski–Kieslowski because I will be able to ascribe it a function later on:

D: (on the phone): Good morning, I'd like to know how the things
             are going on... What do you mean we are not importers? The
             City is importing, the City Mayor. [*He turns on the loudspeaker
             so that I can hear.*]
A woman: You told me that it's Foreign Trade Co. which imports.
D: It does, on orders from the City Office.
W: Well yes, they are importing but we don't have any information...
D: And what kind of information can we give you?
W: What kind of agreement is it, how does it work...
D: Will a copy of the agreement be enough?
W: Yes, please.
D [*to me*]: Have you heard? You haven't heard the beginning. We buy the
             metro cars from Russia, a very high VAT, 25%. Buses and
             trams are VAT exempt. But in order to be exempt from VAT the
             metro cars have to be bought by an administrative unit which
             is exempt from VAT...
FD: It's not clear whether we are talking about a direct import tax
             or VAT.
D: ... but such a unit does not exist. An operational unit which is
             buying these cars will be established only the next year. I
             spoke with the Ministry and I was told that there is no
             problem; it will be done in January. I came back from the sani-
             tarium in March, nobody knew anything. A secretary told me
             that the boss is out, she can't find anything and I should talk
             to a VAT director. The director was very nice – they all want
             nothing else but to help you and settle matters, but he said

that import VAT is somebody else's business. This other director says that if it's import VAT it must be Madam Bartczak. Madam Bartczak says that she doesn't know anything, but if everybody says that it's her office, it must be it. Eventually she rummaged at the bottom of a drawer and she found it there – if I hadn't called she would have never looked in it. I've told her once more that the City Office imports through its import agency. She told me no problem. But just in case I called her again – and you heard yourself. Now she tells me that it's Foreign Trade and not the City Office! So I tell her once more that Foreign Trade is the city office's agency. So she wants to see it on paper...

At this point not much is known: it is a chronicle of events – contemporary (conversations, telephones) – but also of the past. We learn that MCGH had a different structure and organizational identity in the past and that these will be changed presently as a part of a general change in city management caused by the change of political regime (a potential story in its own right). We learn also that on Wednesday some kind of a story must be produced at a conference, and we can guess that various kinds of plots are in the offing, informed by different political interests. FD has his own dream plot: follow the example of the Swiss. Directors suspect both the city and the county of emplotment of their own. By Wednesday, MCGH must arrive with their own story and try to make it win against competitive stories and plots; we do not know yet which. Such a story needs supporting evidence and the Director's telephone conversation was an effort to secure it (story making can be hard work), but it has also served as an instructive story for my benefit: see how chaotic everything is?

Day 3 (Wednesday).

9.30. A car arrives. *D* and I are on our way to press conference (he cancelled his doctor's appointment) when the Technical Director comes in.

TD: What am I supposed to do with that engine driver from St. Petersburg? [*Who was to drive the engine on a trial run of the subway.*]

D: I don't know, it's your engine driver.

TD: Our own engine drivers have never driven this kind of engine and can run into problems.

D: Find some engine drivers on the black job market, or take two engine drivers from Minsk. [*This is what happens in Kieslowski's movie.*]

TD: How can I do such a thing!

D: Do it any way you want, but do not make a big fuss of that engine driver from St. Petersburg, because they will immediately request a cooperation agreement and sure enough there will be a talk in town that the Russians teach us and that we exchange experiences...

TD: Well I know, but how can I use him unofficially...
D: Well maybe not unofficially, but without letting everybody know.
TD: But where do I get another driver...
D: Oh, I don't know.

By saving two bits of action/dialogue (Kislewski's telephone and the allusion to Kieslowski's movie). I can attribute to them a function in my narrative: I can show how people use the contextual material to make sense of their own organizing (Czarniawska, 2000; 2002). But this function is not important for the narrative the directors are making. A story that becomes more and more central for them is the involvement of Russian contractors in the metro construction.

While the Director can permit himself to produce a facetious plot *à la* Kieslowski in the safety of his office ('get two drivers from Minsk if you do not want one from St. Petersburg'), at the press conference the plot is clear and obviously decided together with the Deputy Mayor, who continues to produce anxious cues:

The press conference takes place at the city hall in Bankowy Square. When we enter the room there is one man from *Gazeta Wyborcza* (the main Polish daily) and quite a few women journalists, very young. At 10:04 enters Deputy Mayor and his spokesperson (a woman). More journalists arrive...

Spokeswoman: We have many novelties to present, as we would like to present to press all the fields of activity of city administration. Today is the first part – the metro.

D: It won't be possible neither to complete the metro before the end of the council's term nor to extend the term, but the present council is giving metro a lot... How much? After 12 years we have built 12 km. Some say it's a long time, others say that there were investments which took much more time, and not only in Poland. At any rate, now the political and economic conditions are different and the metro construction can proceed.

Even though it's almost ready there is a lot of work to be done. We don't have all norms ready as it hasn't been decided whether it's a train or a tram, whether the traffic should be left-sided or right-sided, and which of the central institutions will take care of the metro. The number of norms is enormous, and many concern passengers. First of all there are safety norms, of the utmost importance, but also organizational and technical norms are important. What we have for the time being you will find on this page [*He hands out a sheet with technical data and asset distribution: stations, cars and crews.*]

I have to say that even though we have started in a political system which isn't remembered well, we were

	able to modernize, and we have technologies that are second to nobody in the world.
Deputy Mayor:	Mr. Director, can you point out that we supervise car production because many people feel uneasy about it...
D:	Of course! We buy Russian metro cars and we have had problems with their construction and quality of execution. The cars that were originally donated were delivered 3 months after the promised delivery date. We weren't allowed to interfere with production. But according to a new contract, the Polish State Railways carries out the direct operational supervision and already after a few weeks it turned out that there are differences in opinion between our supervisors and their workers. I could say even that there are conflicts, but the management is on our side because they see that this is the only opportunity for the factory to survive.
Deputy Mayor:	But Mr. Director, you have to say explicitly that we have control over what they are doing, because the way you say it sounds like if we didn't know what's going on there.
D:	Why, of course. If they deliver cars that are not finished properly, let's say on Friday, hoping that controllers went for the weekend, our supervisors will see to it that they work on Saturday and Sunday.

The remaining questions concern the dates of the possible opening of the metro; no further issues concerning investors or contractors are mentioned.

The plot is simple – that of conversion: at the beginning of the construction the involvement of the Russians was large; now the political system has changed and the relationship has changed accordingly. Before, Russians were teaching and helping the MCGH; now it is MCGH who teaches and helps the Russians. The Director attempts to weave in his favorite plot – the transformation of MCGH ('although we have started in a political system which is not remembered well') but the Deputy will have none of it: get back to the Russians! Did the emplotment work?

Day 4.

10:23. A journalist from *Gazeta Wyborcza* comes to the Director's office.

D: You didn't write anything about yesterday's press conference. What was the reason? You didn't bother?

J: No, we wrote but...

D: About the press conference but not about the metro.

J: Well I wouldn't know, ... but I have an idea.

D: What kind of idea?

J: Metro construction is almost finished, but it doesn't show, you said it yourself yesterday, it is all under the ground. Therefore our newspaper would like to show it, to show it step by step, to write a reportage.

D: It's fine with me.

J: Of course we will need a leading story.

D: I would suggest following points. First, how we bring specific structures into operation, how investments are converted into operations.
Second, particular stations. Some of them will be esthetically more
interesting than others, some will have very modern escalators, etc.
Third, the delivery of the Russian metro cars – from the border to the
driving tests. You could go to Brest [*border railway station*].

J: Or to St. Petersburg.

D: I can't fix that for you, a contact of course, not the trip.

J: But of course the trip will be paid by the newspaper...

D: Of course I have to inform you that you aren't the only interested, for
example Top Canal [*TV*] shot a few photographs and showed them, it
was very interesting, it looked quite different than how I see it.

J: We as a newspaper don't have such possibilities.

D: But you have a photographer, although frankly, one can hardly see
anything on your pictures.

J: But it will improve...

D: Everybody says that everything will improve, but the fact is, only
Rzeczpospolita and *Zycie Warszawy* have good quality pictures.

J: Don't forget that if a subject is of general interest, for example the
production of the metro cars in St. Petersburg, we can print it on
Friday [Gazeta Wyborcza *publishes on Fridays a weekly supplement
printed on fine paper with colored illustrations and photographs*].

D: I would like also to get something out of it. To settle a thing or two
with your help. I would wish that you weren't only the metro's guest
but also got in touch with authorities such as county administration,
city administration. They have to be taught how to answer the old
questions, why this station is here and not there, why this one was
canceled and that one introduced. After all, the metro will open during
their term in office.

J: We have common interests...

[*The interview continues for an hour or so and, finally, the journalist goes
out. He stops at the door, saying*]: The car production, this is something
I wouldn't like to miss.

D: The Russians will be grateful if you write something nice about them
for a change.

J: It depends very much on what I'll see.

The story has been delivered with a proper kind of emplotment, as far as I
could judge, but its most important audience – the leading newspaper – has
not been listening. Finally, the Director has their representative in his office and
can openly negotiate about their mutual interest. 'The Russian plot', however,
will not be easy. The journalist clearly signals both strong interest and an
unwillingness to buy an already-plotted story: he will have to go to see
for himself in order to decide. Observe that, for him, as for most reporters,

mimesis and character development are much more important than they are for the managers (and, perhaps, for the students of management?).

The emplotment continues. Unlike in a sports broadcast, the chronicle is not very important. Mimesis (the way of describing events) is a means of selling a given type of plot, but the plot is central. The battle of emplotment is a power battle: it is the old saying that it is the victors who write history.

EXERCISES

Exercise 2.1: multiple identities

Try to emplot your biography in three different ways (possible plots: 'The quest for knowledge', 'Success story'; possible genres: Romance, Comedy, Satire). Do not go to Exercise 2.2 until the task is completed.

Exercise 2.2: life stories

Reflect on the work that went into changing your biography into a story with a plot. Where did the plots come from? Your fantasy? Media? Your family history? What changes in structure (omissions, completions) were needed to achieve the plot? Has mimesis (the descriptions) changed with the various plots?

Exercise 2.3: observing how stories are made

Take as a starting point any event reported in the media from the time it happened. Watch and note down how it is being made into a story: are there competing plots? What means are used to saturate the event with meaning? Whose story wins at the time you end your observation?

FURTHER READING

Linde, Charlotte (1993) *Life Stories. The Creation of Coherence.* Oxford: Oxford University Press.
Shotter, John, and Gergen, Kenneth J. (eds) (1989) *Texts of Identity.* London: Sage.
Sköldberg, Kaj (2002) *The Poetic Logic of Administration. Styles and Changes of Style in the Art of Organizing.* London: Routledge.

Notes

1   As every reader of Jane Austen knows, Wickham was the wicked one.
2   Richard Harvey Brown (1998) postulates that this genre, and the trope of irony, is best suited for social sciences (see also Chapter 10).
3   At that time, Kieslowski's *Three Colors: White* (a film about Warsaw under the new regime) had been released.

3

Collecting Stories

Oral history

For history, ethnology, and cultural anthropology, the narrative turn was a novelty only insofar as it applied to their own writings (I will return to this topic in Chapters 8 and 9). Stories as one kind of field material were no news to them. Oral history – of families, communities, and societies – relies upon the collection of stories (Paul Thompson, 1978). The famous *The Making of the English Working Class* (by E.P. Thompson, 1963) was based on a collection of reports by paid government informants in the early nineteenth century. Paolo Apolito's relation concerning apparitions of the Madonna in Campania, Italy (1990/1998), was originally entitled 'It's been said that they have seen Madonna' – not a felicitous phrase in English but pointing toward 'circulation of stories' as an important element in a community's life. As Paul Connerton expressed it in his *How Societies Remember*, 'The production of more or less *informally* told narrative histories turns out to be basic activity for characterisation of human actions. It is a feature of all communal memory' (1989: 16–17).

Much as the folklore scholars would agree with all these statements (see, e.g., Narayan and George, 2002), a student of contemporary western society might have objections. Isn't oral history something exotic or something from the distant past, rudimental and unimportant in modern, literate societies?

Comparative studies of literate and non-literate societies (Goody, 1986) show that, while narratives exist in both oral and literate cultures, there are indeed three forms of text which became possible only due to the existence of the script: tables, lists, and recipes. The first two differ from the narrative in that they present items of information in a disjointed, abstract way. In order to memorize a list or a table, a mnemonic device is required to make up for the lack of connections. The recipe assumes a chronological connection and thus seems to resemble a narrative, but it lacks the propelling force of a cause or an intention – the plot of the narrative. Clouds lead to rain and greed leads to crime; sifting the flour does not lead to breaking eggs. The recipe fulfills the learning function of the narrative in that it provides the learner with a vicarious experience – but in a way that is closer to that of tables or lists. One could say that recipes are lists, but of actions, not of objects.

In his *Foucault's Pendulum* (1989), Umberto Eco provides an amusing illustration of one difference between lists and narratives. In his story, the Rosicrucians, with the enthusiastic researchers – Casaubon, Belbo, and Diotallevi – on their heels, were presented with an old parchment from Provins (Provence), which contained the following text:

> *a la ... Saint Jean*
> *36 p charrete de fein*
> *6 ... entiers avec saiel*
> *p ... les blanc mantiax*
> *r ... s ... chevaliers de Pruins pour la ... j.nc*
> *6 foiz 6 en places*
> *chascune foiz 20 a ... 120 a ...*
> *iceste est l'ordonation*
> *al donjon li premiers*
> *it li secunz joste iceus qui ... pans*
> *it al refuge*
> *it a Nostre Dame de l'altre part de l'iau*
> *it a l'ostel des popelicans*
> *it a la pierre*
> *3 foiz 6 avant la feste ... la Grand Pute.* (Eco, 1989: 135)

They reconstructed it as a great PLAN of the Templar Knights, seeking revenge against their enemies in the centuries to come:

THE (NIGHT OF) SAINT JOHN
36 (YEARS) P(OST) HAY WAIN
6 (MESSAGES) INTACT WITH SEAL
F(OR THE KNIGHTS WITH) THE WHITE CLOAKS [TEMPLARS]
R(ELAP)S(I) OF PROVINS FOR (VAIN)JANCE [REVENGE]
6 TIMES IN 6 PLACES
EACH TIME 20 Y(EARS MAKES) 120 Y(EARS)
THIS IS THE PLAN
THE FIRST GO TO THE CASTLE
IT(ERUM) [AGAIN AFTER 120 YEARS] THE SECOND JOIN THOSE (OF THE) BREAD
AGAIN TO THE REFUGE

AGAIN TO OUR LADY BEYOND THE RIVER
AGAIN TO THE HOSTEL OF POPELICANS
AGAIN TO THE STONE
3 TIMES 6 [666] BEFORE THE FEAST (OF THE) GREAT WHORE. (Eco, 1989: 135–6)

Casaubon's girlfriend, Lia, a researcher in her own right, reads it very differently and with much better support in the sources. According to her, it is a simple shopping (or, rather, selling) list containing a merchant's order for cloth and roses, Provins' most important products at that time:

In Rue Saint Jean:
36 sous for wagons of hay.
Six new lengths of cloth with seal
to rue des Blancs-Manteaux.
Crusaders' roses to make a jonchée:
six bunches of six in the six following places,
each 20 deniers, making 120 deniers in all.
Here is the order:
the first to the Fort
item the second to those in Porte-aux-Pains
item to the Church of the Refuge
item to the Church of Notre Dame, across the river
item to the old building of the Cathars
item to rue de La Pierre-Ronde.
And three bunches of six before the feast, in the whore's street.

Because they, too, poor things, maybe wanted to celebrate the feast day by making themselves nice little hats of roses. (Eco, 1989: 536)

But this sober reading comes too late: the three males have already launched themselves into mortal danger because of their belief in the Plan. Eco's point concerns the dangers of overinterpretation (I return to this issue in Chapter 5). But he also shows how dedicated they are to their story: Lia's prosaic list cannot compete with the allure of a narrative.

Yet modern organizations are not supposed to be alluring but sober; and tables, lists, and recipes are undoubtedly the modern props of knowledge. Formal organizations, those epitomes of rationalized collective action, are often presented as sites where narrative has no role for learning and memory, at least within programmatic attempts to influence organizational learning. Tables and lists (many 'models' and taxonomies are complicated lists) are given priority as teaching aids in schools as well as in companies. Again, while they can fulfill certain functions that narratives cannot, the reverse applies even more. Almost certainly the greater part of societal learning happens through the circulation of stories (Weick, 1995; Orr, 1996). Also, the extent to which the modern props of learning – and the technologies of writing which support them – are used in modern organizations varies. My studies of city management revealed, for example, that in the Stockholm city office many important deals were made on the phone, whereas in Warsaw every agreement had to be confirmed in writing. Stockholm, however, was flooded with leaflets, brochures, and memos, whereas in Warsaw there were very few of these and important information was conveyed face to face only. Oral cultures are not necessarily ages away. As Goody and Watt (1968) observed, the oral tradition remains the primary mode of cultural orientation even in a literate culture, which is rather fortunate in light of the unlimited variety and fragmentation of the written sources available. And the oral tradition depends on the narrative.

Each field of practice (including the practice of research) has, at any point in time, a series of stories in circulation. They might concern recent events that are in need of emplotment or, to the contrary, be focused on a distant history, giving coherence and legitimacy to the field of practice as it is today. Each family has a repertoire of such stories. They are offered to newcomers as the means of introduction to a community, but they are also repeated in the presence of the very actors who participated in the event, thus consolidating a community feeling by reifying its history. Many of them have a quasi-mythical character and are exploited in similar fashion, as described in many an anthropological study. This chapter explains the pragmatic functions of such stories and quotes well-known examples of studies based on story collection.

Collecting stories

In the light of what was said above about the role of stories in learning and memory, it is perhaps not surprising that one of the earliest studies of modern phenomena that relied on story collection came from the field of education. Burton R. Clark (1972) studied three famous US colleges (Reed, Antioch, and Swarthmore) and in all these places discovered a story in circulation that was rooted in history, claimed unique accomplishment, and was held in warm regard by the group who was recalling it. He called these stories 'organizational sagas':

> Saga, originally referring to a medieval Icelandic or Norse account of achievements and events in the history of a person or a group, has come to mean a narrative of heroic exploits, of a unique development that has deeply stirred the emotions of participants and descendants. Thus a saga is not simply a story but a story that at some time has had a particular base of believers … The element of belief is crucial, for without the credible story, the events and persons become history; with the development of belief, a particular bit of history becomes a definition full of pride and identity for the group. (Clark, 1972: 178)

All three sagas fulfilled the same (symbolic) function but they differed in plot. The Reed College saga told the story of creative acts performed by a pioneer-like leader in an (educational) desert. The Antioch College saga was the story of an established organization in deep crisis, saved by a Utopian reformer. The Swarthmore College saga was a story of a successful organization that was in danger of succumbing to complacency, until rescued by a leader sensitive to the winds of change.

Although the basic plot varied, the central Character remained the same. Indeed, modern stories tend to reproduce the masculine domination, offering few, if any, counterparts of folklore stories about witches and wise women. This characteristic is not limited to heroic sagas where the presence of charismatic leaders is a part of the classical plot. Anthropologists Sabine Helmers and Regina Buhr (1994) carried out a field study in a large German company producing typewriters. They spent three weeks in the company, conducting interviews and observing. During their stay several interlocutors, all men, told them the following story:

The Tactful Typewriter Mechanic

The new secretary had called in the mechanic many times because her electric typewriter kept making spaces where they didn't belong. After trying unsuccessfully to find the cause, the mechanic decided to observe the secretary at work for a while. He soon discovered the problem. The girl, generously endowed with feminine attractions, kept hitting the space key involuntarily every time she bent forward. The mechanic showed that he was capable of dealing with this rather delicate situation. He found the excuse to send her out of the office and raised her swivel chair four centimeters. Since then she had no problems with her machine and has nothing but praise for the excellent mechanic. (Helmers and Buhr, 1994: 176)

At first, say Helmers and Buhr, they did not pay much attention to the story but its repetitions made them curious. The story was told as if the event took place the day before, but the attempt to trace it led them to an Austrian in-house publication for a typewriter dealer dated 2 June 1963 (the excerpt is quoted as from that source). Thus a practically ancient story was kept alive by retelling it and was given relevance by situating it contemporarily and in the narrators' own company. The tale had its 'sisters' in other companies, industries, countries, and times. Helmers and Buhr were able to show that such stereotyping of women as 'dumb blondes' actually hampered technological developments in the typewriter industry. Stories of the kind they encountered redefined many technically solvable machine errors as 'users' problems'.

The title of this chapter might be somewhat misleading: 'collecting stories' sounds like a passive occupation, stories waiting like mushrooms to be picked. In fact, Boland and Tenkasi (1995) were worried that too many researchers expected exactly that. Boland and Tenkasi took a highly critical view of 'collecting' organizational narratives as if they were artifacts for ever petrified in organizational reality waiting to be 'discovered' by a researcher. Yet every narrative becomes new with each retelling, and the 'petrification' of stories is not the result of the myopia of the researcher but of intensive stabilizing work by the narrators, some examples of which we saw in Chapter 2. Nevertheless, story collection needs to be supported by the study of narrative performances, such as undertaken by David Boje (1991).

Telling stories

Boje took inspiration from studies of Harvey Sacks (1992) and his followers, who investigated the occurrence of stories in conversations.[1] One context especially rich for the story-carrying conversation was, he observed, a work organization:

> In organizations, storytelling is the preferred sense-making currency of human relationships among internal and external stakeholders. People engage in a dynamic process of incremental refinement of their stories of new events as well as on-going interpretations of culturally sacred story lines. When a decision is at hand, the old stories are recounted and compared to an unfolding story line to keep the organizations from repeating historically bad choices and to invite the repetition of past successes. In a turbulent environment, the organization halls and offices pulsate with a story life of the here and now that is richer and more vibrant than the firm's environments.
>
> Even in stable times, the story is highly variable and sometimes political, in that part of the collective processing involves telling different versions of stories to different audiences ... Each performance is never the completed story; it is an unraveling process of confirming new data and new interpretations as these become part of an unfolding story line. (Boje, 1991: 106)

Boje thus set out to record everyday conversations in a large office-supply firm he was studying in order to capture spontaneous storytelling episodes. He then used the program ETHNOGRAPH to code the over 100 hours of tape recordings, a procedure that took him 400 hours. His findings concerned two aspects of storytelling: how they occur in conversations and in what way they are used. As far as the first aspect is concerned, Boje discovered that storytelling in contemporary organizations hardly follows the traditional pattern of a narrator telling a story from the beginning to the end in front of an enchanted and attentive audience. Narrators told their stories in bits and pieces, were often interrupted, sometimes for the purpose of complementing the story, and sometimes for aborting the storytelling. As to uses to which stories were put, Boje classified them into pattern finding, pattern elaboration, and pattern fitting. This classification exemplifies well Karl Weick's insights concerning sensemaking (1995). A story is a frame – a frame that emerges and is tried out, a frame that is developed and elaborated, or a frame that can easily absorb the new event.

Boje's study shows that the line between 'story making' and 'story collecting', topics of two separate chapters in this book, is very fine if it exists at all. The structuring of this book does not correspond to the 'structure of reality', as it were; it is a device used to structure a text. Also, although both Boje's and Gabriel's (see the next section) studies were done in workplaces, storytelling is not limited to such sites. Family is an obvious site for storytelling, as are playgroups and various associations. Still, the 'work-worlds' may deserve special attention.

The concept of a 'work-world' is inspired by Benita Luckmann (1978), who pointed out that the lifeworld of modern people is divided into segments or subuniverses. One such small lifeworld of a modern person is a world of work, the other two being family and ecological community (the list should now be extended to include virtual communities). Accepting her reading means a deviation from the common viewpoint that workplaces are ruled by the rigid arm of the 'system' and hence stand in opposition to the 'lifeworld'.[2] Luckmann demonstrated two interesting traits of such 'small lifeworlds': one, that they are surprisingly similar to traditional communities; and, two, that the main difference between 'the modern person' and his or her traditional equivalent is that there are several such worlds in modernity which requires (but also permits) frequent 'gear shifting'. The stories circulate in all, although gear shifting might also mean genre shifting.

Luckmann's idea found an excellent illustration in Julian E. Orr's (1996) ethnography of the work of technicians who repair copying machines. While employed by a big corporation, the technicians practically managed to ignore it. They conceived their job – in the sense of a work practice rather than a relation of employment and hierarchy – as an individual, challenging task, made possible by a supportive community. The community was a context where 'war stories' were swapped and where the collective knowledge was produced, maintained, and distributed. Orr concludes that:

> the skilled practice of field service work [is] necessarily improvised…, and centered on the creation and maintenance of control and understanding. Control and understanding are achieved through a coherent account of the situation, requiring both diagnostic and narrative skills. Understanding is maintained through circulation of this knowledge by retelling the narratives to other members of the community, and this preservation of understanding contributes to the maintenance of control. (1996: 161)

Orr is very clear on one point: the stories are not *about* work, they *are* the work of the technicians, even though they may create other outcomes:

when technicians gather, their conversation is full of talk about machines. This talk shows their understanding of the world of service; in another sense, the talk creates that world and even creates the identities of the technicians themselves. But neither talk nor identity is the goal of technicians' practice. The goal is getting the job done, keeping the customers happy, and keeping the machines running. (1996: 161)

The technicians' stories are not 'organizational stories'; they are 'stories that organize' (Czarniawska and Gagliardi, 2003). Most likely, the storytelling registered by Boje (1991) fulfilled similar functions, although he focused more on their formal role in the sensemaking process. What makes the difference between storytelling as reported by Boje and Orr and that described by Gabriel (see the next section) is that those 'work stories' are of a doubtful aesthetic or political value and are often elliptic and difficult to understand for a bystander. 'Organizational stories', on the other hand, seem to be meant for a general audience and – although no doubt fulfilling multiple functions – can hardly be of practical use for a problem at hand.

Stories in and about organizations

Yiannis Gabriel (2000) begins his book with a confession: he is a story lover, and it is a love story that dates from his childhood and carries into his family life. For a long time, however, he saw storytelling and working life, and especially working life consisting of doing research on working life, as two separate domains. Both as an employee and as a researcher, however, he was struck by two observations. First of all, different people told him the same, or very similar, story, as if they had rehearsed it beforehand. Secondly, long after his working experience or his research had ended, these stories remained in his memory longer than facts and people. Hence his present effort, although inspired by folklore research, aimed at answering three questions:

1. How can we study organizations through the stories that are told in them and about them?
2. What do stories tell us about the nature of organizations as distinct forms of human collectivity?
3. What do stories encountered in organizations tell us about the nature and functions of storytelling? (Gabriel, 2000: 2)

I am quoting these questions verbatim as a kind of warning. Many young scholars, fascinated by the presence of stories, proceed to do studies that show this presence. This is not enough; besides, it has already been done as documented not least by examples I am quoting here. A similar phenomenon happened in economics, according to Robert Solow (1988), when the economists were informed (mostly by Deirdre McCloskey, 1985) that economics uses metaphors in its writings. The result was a series of studies that Solow summarizes as 'Look, Ma, there is a metaphor!' studies. The same thing is taking place in narrative studies: many of them are of the 'Look, Ma, there is a narrative!' type. Yet pointing out that science uses stories and metaphors, and so do other types of human activities, cannot be the whole program. The point is: what are the consequences of scientific rhetoric and what are the consequences of storytelling – for those who tell the stories and those who study them?

Gabriel adopts a narrow definition of the story, such as the one I took on in Chapter 2, and contrasts stories with other common types of organizational narratives: opinions and reports (the latter clearly a modern version of a chronicle; see Chapter 2). Here is an example of a complete story that is worth repeating for its entertainment value:

> There was a chap driving a lorry and he hit a cat so he got out of the lorry and saw this cat on the side of the road and thought I'd better finish it off ... smashed it over the head, got back in and drove off. A lady or a chap phoned the police and said I've just seen a Board lorry driver get out and kill my cat. So they chased after the van and found it and asked the driver whether he had killed the cat so he said he had run over it and couldn't leave it like that ... it's cruel so I finished it off. So they said can we examine your van and he said yes by all means so they examined the van and found a dead cat under the wheel arch. So it was the wrong cat [he had killed] sleeping at the side of the road. (Gabriel, 2000: 23)

Gabriel points out that it does not make sense to check the veracity of the story, and treats it as an example of organizational folklore.[3] I would like to point out that, like the story of a tactful mechanic, it contains many a message about Board company. It is not the plot (a comic road story involving a case of mistaken identity) but the *mimesis* that carries the message: we learn that Board drivers are people sensitive to the suffering of animals and that the British police force reacts promptly even to extremely exotic complaints with exceptional thoroughness and alacrity.

Gabriel then moves to inspecting 'the ways the stories are made', showing how the same incident involving the explosion of a fire extinguisher takes the form of four different stories. He proceeds to trace the poetic tropes at work in story making in a way inspired by White and resembling that of Sköldberg (Chapter 2). He gives examples of an epic story, a tragic story, and a comic story (he has not found a romantic tale) and proceeds to analyze them according to five features: (1) a protagonist; (2) a predicament; (3) attempts to resolve the predicament; (4) the outcome of these attempts; and (5) the reactions of the protagonist (p. 61). This kind of structural analysis will be given more attention in Chapter 7; for now, we will look for the answers to Gabriel's questions.

Surprisingly enough, Gabriel is more pessimistic about story-based research than his own text. In a somewhat mournful ending, he says:

Unlike the café and the pub, the village square and the family table, organizations do not appear to be a natural habitat of storytelling – after all most people in organizations are too busy appearing to be busy to be able to engage in storytelling. Nor is trust, respect, and love among members of organizations such as to encourage free and uninhibited narration. Moreover, stories in organizations compete against other narrativities, especially against information and data, but also against clichés, platitudes, acronyms, artefacts small and large, arguments, opinions, and so forth. In such an environment, amidst the noisy din of facts, numbers and images, the delicate, time-consuming discourse of storytelling is easily ignored or silenced. Few organizations are spontaneous storytelling cultures. (2000: 240)

As a worker daily drowned in the ocean of repetitive stories, I almost wish Gabriel was right. As his reader, I think Gabriel is using a *hyperbole* – a self-conscious exaggeration (Lanham, 1991: 86). The quotation continues: 'Yet, there *is* storytelling going on in organizations, and some organizational stories are good stories.' And the bulk of his book shows how revealing the study of stories actually is (on the matter of whether I have the right to go against an author's explicitly stated intentions, see Chapter 5).

To begin with, the stories he found were not few: 130 interviews gave rise to 404 stories. (Gabriel also gives useful advice in such practical matters as eliciting and collecting stories.) The following analysis of stories[4] elucidates several extremely important and often otherwise hidden aspects of social life. One such aspect is the role stories play in the drama of organizational power and resistance, at which I hinted in the previous chapter. Another is that stories permit access to the emotional life of organizations. This topic has been taken up by other writers (see a collection edited by Fineman, 1993), but Gabriel addresses a highly original aspect: stories as revealing the nostalgia present in organizations. A third aspect, closely related, is the religious side of organizing: Gabriel offers a compelling interpretation of the longevity of the leader-as-a-hero kind of plot – the leader is a kind of surrogate God in organizations: 'By highlighting the untypical, the critical, the extraordinary, stories give us access to what lies beyond the normal and the mundane' (2000: 240). Gabriel speaks here in tune with Jerome Bruner, who pointed out that 'The function of the narrative is to find an intentional state that mitigates, or at least makes comprehensible, a deviation from a canonical cultural pattern' (1990: 49–50). Thus stories might not tell all about work-worlds, but they do tell a lot.

Ways of story collecting

The literature on story collecting reveals at least three main ways of collecting stories. The first is the one used by Boje and Orr: recording of spontaneous incidents of storytelling during prolonged field research. As pointed out by

Gabriel, this is not easy: it requires a special sensibility (which can be acquired, however, in the field), a good memory, or a skillful and unobtrusive use of recording devices.

The second approach is the one used by Gabriel himself: eliciting stories. Looking at his interview guide, I was struck by its similarity to Flanagan's critical incidents technique (1954). This technique has been invented within an approach very distant from a narrative one and yet nothing says it cannot be used for that purpose.

This particular technique originated in the Aviation Psychology Program of the US Army Air Forces in World War II, with the specific purpose of developing procedures for the selection and classification of aircrews. Flanagan asked pilots to tell him about critical incidents in their service.

Flanagan defined an incident as an observable human activity that can be seen as a whole: it has a beginning and an end, even if it can be related to many other, earlier and later activities. A critical incident is an incident that is untypical in the sense of not happening regularly, even if typical for a given type of activity (and therefore, for example, an activity repeated several times every day is not a critical incident). It must, however, be important from the point of view of the main activity of processes taking place in the site under study. Both judgments (untypical, important) must be made by the observer under the guidance of the researcher.

The procedure (usually an interview but also an observation technique) should cover the following steps:

1   Establishing general aims of an activity. (Researchers who believe, like Karl Weick, that aims of an activity are best discovered specifically and post factum might replace it with a question concerning the type of activity.)
2   Describing the unit and the actors. (Again, Flanagan has clearly in mind formal organizations. Researchers who study other type of communities will be satisfied with a description of a site at which the activity takes place. A good description should resemble stage specifications, so that it is clear where are the doors and where are the windows – metaphorically speaking – what costumes should actors wear, etc.)
3   Choosing an incident. During an interview, the interviewer and the interviewee make the choice together. During an observation, the observer decides and justifies the choice.
4   Description of the critical incident. Again, it should resemble a play script. It must be chronologically ordered, detailed (everything of importance for understanding the whole), and complete with the intentions of actors (as declared by themselves or attributed by the observer).
5   Critical judgments of the observer may be included but must be clearly separated.

This description of the procedure makes it clear that the resulting account might well be a story or a chronicle. Unless the study aims at storytelling specifically, it does not matter much as chronicles and other types of narratives are also texts permitting interesting interpretations.

The third way of collecting stories is to ask for them. Much as I focus in this chapter on oral histories, written stories are also created and circulated, not least in the new medium of the Internet. Accordingly, I used such an approach (which is still a variation of Flanagan's technique) in a study on power in organizations. Students of management, psychology, and sociology in different countries were given the following instruction:

Name or pseudonym:
Age:
Gender:

Power is one of the phenomena that always interested social scientists, were they philosophers or organization theorists. Nevertheless, we do not really know what power looks like in concrete, contemporary organizations. Please think for a moment about an incident involving organizational power that you recently observed. Take some time now, before reading further, to remember the details of that incident.

Now please describe, as fully as possible, the details of that incident, explaining the situation that led to the incident, the people involved, what was said and done by whom, and the consequences of the incident. Take as many additional pages as you wish.

Why have you chosen this particular incident? Could you comment on organizational power as you see it and as it is described in your incident? Thank you very much for your cooperation!

This instruction resulted in a whole collection of very interesting stories.[5] Monika Kostera uses a similar technique (2002), sometimes changing it so that, instead of a theme, the respondents are asked to complete a story of which they are given the first line ('You are free to go, said the Managing Director'). She also asked managers to write short poems and they obliged her (Kostera, 1997). Scheytt et al. (2003) applied the same instruction in a study of the notion of 'control' in different cultures.

The choice of a specific technique depends on opportunities, personal talents, and preferences. Throughout this book I avoid giving specific recipes (I prefer to quote stories) because most prescriptions, sensible as they were in a given context of use, can easily turn absurd in another one. If there is one general rule of field research it is that all techniques must be context sensitive. A field researcher is constantly making decisions as to the next step to take (not least moral decisions), and there is no authority in the academic word who could foresee all contexts and all occurrences.

The point I was trying to make in this chapter is that *long-lived narratives, especially stories, are sediments of norms and practices and, as such, deserve careful attention.* Each workplace, each group and community has a contemporary and historical repertoire of stories, sometimes divided into 'internal stories' and 'external stories', sometimes stories spread abroad with a hope of their return in a more legitimate form – for example, via mass media (Kunda, 1992).

Boland and Tenkasi (1995) have made an important point, however. Stories do not lie around – they are fabricated, circulated, and contradicted. Using an industrial metaphor (following Michel de Certeau, 1984), it could be said that stories are produced (concocted, fabricated), sold (told, circulated), and consumed (listened to, read, interpreted) – often all in the same performance. Nor is a story collector, in this case a researcher, a mushroom picker: he or she listens selectively, remembers fragmentarily, and re-counts in a way that suits his or her purpose. Interestingly enough, all these phenomena can be observed in one type of interaction: an interview.

EXERCISES

Exercise 3.1: family or workplace story

Does your family have a story that is often told when guests are around? (This notion encompasses strangers as well as visiting family members.) If not, can you recall a story that is told to visitors at your workplace? Perhaps you remember stories told to you when you were a new employee? Write up whichever story is easier to retrieve.

Exercise 3.2: collective storytelling

Show your story to another family member or to a colleague at work. Ask him or her whether you remembered it well and ask him or her to correct your story on paper (make sure the story is double spaced). Compare the two versions. What do the corrections say about yourself? About your family member or your colleague? What does the story say about your family or about your workplace?

FURTHER READING

Boje, David M. (1991) 'The storytelling organization: a study of story performance in an office-supply firm,' *Administrative Studies Quarterly*, 36: 106–26.
Gabriel, Yiannis (2000) *Storytelling in Organizations: Facts, Fictions and Fantasies*. Oxford: Oxford University Press.
Orr, Julian E. (1996) *Talking about Machines. An Ethnography of a Modern Job*. Ithaca, NY: Cornell University Press.

Notes

1   The reader might wonder how David Boje was able in 1991 to partake in the insights of Sacks' book published in 1992. Sacks' complete *Lectures on Conversation* were first published in 1992, 17 years after his tragic death, but circulated as paper copies of the transcriptions made by Gail Jefferson, and some of them were published separately before 1992.
2   'System' and 'lifeworld' are Husserl's terms, used much by Alfred Schütz and his disciples.
3   Gabriel points out that the notion of organizational folklore (cultural practices and artefacts that are symbolic, spontaneous, and repetitive) has not received much attention from organizational scholars. I agree with him that this is highly regrettable as all kinds of bodily practices and artefacts are powerful carriers of social memory (Connerton, 1989). I suppose the reason is that they are very difficult to study and require a special kind of trained sensitivity, not part of the usual curricula for social science researchers.
4   Gabriel, like Boje, used a computer program: Cardbox-Plus.
5   The results of this study can be found in Czarniawska-Joerges and Kranas (1991), Czarniawska-Joerges (1994) and Czarniawska (2003b); see also Chapter 7.

4

Narratives in an Interview Situation

What is an interview?

The ingenious spelling of the title of Steinar Kvale's book (*InterViews*, 1996) brought to the attention of researchers like myself at least two unpleasant insights about their favorite technique. The first concerned what, in its usual form, an interview is not: *it is not a mutual exchange of views*. A more correct name would be, perhaps, an 'inquisition' or an 'interrogation', quite in tune with the deplorable tradition of calling the interviewees 'informants'. The second insight concerned what, in its frequent version, an interview unfortunately is: collecting views and opinions on whatever topic is mentioned. If an interview is not a part of an opinion survey, this is not what researchers are after: they want to know facts, or attitudes, or many other things outside the interview, the 'reality behind it', as it were.

But *should* a research interview be an exchange of views between the two parties? Kvale takes up a normative, philosophical perspective and claims that, as conversations are the main mode of knowledge production in our societies, the model of conversation, especially its version known as a philosophical dialogue, should become the model for interviews. An interview is two persons seeking knowledge and understanding in a common conversational endeavor.

As long as this postulate is crafted in theoretical terms, there is no need to raise any objections to such an ideal although, semantically speaking, this is a definition of a dialogue, not of an interview. An interview is, indeed, a common enterprise in knowledge production. The practice of research interviewing, however, creates its own complications. Kvale is the first to notice that what he calls a 'professional interview' assumes a power asymmetry: the 'professional' interrogates the 'object' or, in psychological parlance, the 'subject', who responds to the best of his or her knowledge. No wonder that graduate students, at least in Sweden, used to call their interlocutors 'the interview victims'.

There is, however, a peculiar symmetry to this asymmetry. First of all, it is unrealistic to think about a researcher in terms of an omniscient professional. She or he might be professional in her or his own profession (that is, research) but not in the profession of the interlocutor, whose profession is the topic of the conversation. This point is especially obvious in life stories, where the narrators are the only experts on the question of their own lives. The 'power of knowledge', if not other types of power, lies on the side of the interviewee. What the researchers have to offer in exchange is not their views but their respectful and interested attention.

It happens quite often that an interviewed person demands to know the opinion of the interviewer, or the science she or he represents, on the matter in question. But woe to those who take it literally. In most cases, it is either a political trap (the interviewee wants to enlist the researcher on his or her side in an ongoing conflict) or a simple rhetorical diving board. I must admit that I have fallen into this trap many a time and started to expand on my views on the matter only to notice the impatience with which my interlocutor waited for me to end my peroration and give him or her the floor.

The experience of 30 years' interviewing in four countries taught me that practitioners, especially those in elevated positions, are often quite lonely in their thoughts. Every exposition of their thinking within their own organizations has political and practical consequences: others listen, draw conclusions, and act accordingly. There is also a limit to the amount of 'thinking aloud' that even the most loving family can take during the dinner hour. A research interview thus opens a possibility for an unusual but symmetrical exchange. The practitioners offer a personal insight into the realities of their practice. The researchers offer that which our profession has an abundance of but others do not: an opportunity of trying out one's thoughts without practical consequences.

This still does not resolve the second doubt I raised at the outset. Are personal insights and subjective views all that an interview will yield a researcher? The symmetrical situation described above can be satisfactory to a therapist, but should it be acceptable to a researcher?

Another vain hope connected to an interview situation is that it will yield 'information', 'facts'. I understood just how vain that hope was in my study of a reform in Swedish municipalities (Czarniawska, 1988). I asked a simple question (I thought) about the beginning of the reform. I received answers that located it anywhere from the early 1930s to the late 1970s. It was valuable information but not of the kind I expected. To begin with, an unaided memory always falters: people do not remember dates and numbers. There are documents where such facts can be found (always with the caveat that their production must be carefully examined). Further, what people present in the interviews is but the results of their perception, their interpretation of the world, which is of extreme value to the researcher because one may assume that it is the same perception that informs their actions. In this light, the reform that was prepared in the 1930s belongs to a whole different world of meaning from the reform that started in the 1970s; it indicates that those people were in fact implementing different reforms.

It is important to understand that interviews do not stand for anything else; they represent nothing else but themselves. An interview is an interaction that becomes recorded, or inscribed, and this is what it stands for. Such a pitiless definition of an interview situation, however, worries many a researcher. Of what value is an interaction between a researcher and a practitioner?

In social studies this value is quite obvious. An interview is not a window on social reality but it is a part, a sample of that reality. An interaction where a practitioner is submitted to questioning from an external source is typical, in the sense of being frequent, of the work of many people who, in a world of many and fast connections, have constantly to explain themselves to strangers: people from the overseas division, from another department, from the audit office, from a newspaper. We live in an 'interview society' (Atkinson and Silverman, 1997; Gubrium and Holstein, 2002). While each one of these accounts will be unique in the way every interaction is, it would be both presumptuous and unrealistic to assume that a practitioner will invent a whole new story just for the sake of a particular researcher who happened to interview him or her. The narratives are well rehearsed and crafted in a legitimate logic. This 'logic of representation' might be another problem, and I will return to it later.

An interview as an interaction and as a narrative production site

David Silverman's approach to interviews based on the insights of symbolic interactionism can be very helpful to desperate researchers. He pointed out that an interview can be treated as an observation of an interaction between the two people in question (Silverman, 2001). Silverman goes further than the classic interactionists, challenging the quasi-naturalist assumptions made by symbolic interactionism and suggesting sensitive ways of minimizing many traps connected with an overconfidence in the interview as a 'natural' interaction.

One such commonsensical but immensely valuable measure is to make the interviews accompany direct observation, a recommendation often made by ethnographers (see, e.g., Hammersley and Atkinson, 1995). Not only is there then a shared experience to which both interlocutors can easily refer but also it makes it much easier for the interviewer to visualize the stage on which the reported events are taking place, which greatly enhances understanding. Seeing a scene previously described by someone always makes one realize how many cues we lose in our exaggerated reliance on verbal reports. This realization leads more and more researchers to use video equipment whenever possible, although videotaping exacts its price in making the observation more obtrusive. But, if I may add in passing, there are no entirely unobtrusive methods; indeed, there is no reason to expect that researchers can get a 'free ride' in the social world. Every interaction has its price – and it is a part of the duty of each member of society to pay as demanded.

An interview can thus be treated as a recorded interaction and then analyzed with such assistance as conversation analysis (see, e.g., Edwards and Lampert, 1993; Psathas, 1995; ten Have, 1998; Silverman, 2001). Here I would like to point out yet another possibility offered by interviews, inasmuch as they can be steered away from a monologue containing general views on abstract matters. Such an interview may become more like a manipulated conversation, where the manipulation is acknowledged and accepted by both parties. Such conversations might be a rich source of knowledge about social practice insofar as they produce narratives. Here I return to a wider meaning of the term 'narrative' that includes stories, but also chronicles (or reports, as Gabriel, 2000, calls them).

During an interview, an interviewee may retell narratives that circulate on a given site of practice, or the interview itself may become a site for a narrative production. Prompted by the researcher, a practitioner may concoct a narrative, thereby revealing to the researcher the narrative devices in practical use. Indeed, it is highly unlikely that the interviewee should resort to a repertoire of narrative devices unusual for his or her practice.

Miller and Glassner point out that 'interviewees sometimes respond to interviewers through the use of familiar narrative constructs, rather than by providing meaningful insights into their subjective view' (1997: 101). It is 'rather than' I want to contest, much as I am in sympathy with the authors' general stance. 'Meaningful insights into subjective views' can only be expressed by 'familiar narrative constructs' (although this expression may take the form of deviating from or subverting these constructs), otherwise they could not be understood or even recognized as such. We all live and communicate thanks to the incessant use of a widely accessible (rather than 'shared') cultural repertoire. People are using plots they learned from films and TV series (not to forget fairytales) to emplot their own narratives, as we have seen in Chapter 2. This does not make them 'cultural dupes' because they created this repertoire themselves and, if not they, their parents did. This paradox has already been powerfully formulated by Berger and Luckmann (1966): we create 'culture' so that it can create us.

The difference between 'meaningful personal insights' and 'familiar narrative constructs' lies mainly in the interest of the researchers. Individual life histories are unique compositions of materials accessible in the common repertoire, but it is this uniqueness that is of interest to a student of personal narratives (Riessman, 1993). What is a figure for Catherine Riessman is for me a background, and vice versa. Organizational stories delimit a dominant, or a legitimate, range of such compositions in a given time and place, and thus it is their familiarity, their repetitiveness, that is of interest to a student of organizing.

For all these reasons, it is possible to see each community as a site of narrative production, among many other things it may produce. An interview can thus become a micro-site of such production or just a site of distribution where a researcher is allowed to partake in narratives previously produced. This does not mean that research interviews always evoke narratives; unlike spontaneous conversation, they may incite a conscious avoidance of narratives insofar as they are constructed as arenas where only logico-scientific knowledge can be legitimately produced. It is then the task of the interviewer to 'activate narrative production' (Holstein and Gubrium, 1997: 123).

Difficulties connected to eliciting narratives in an interview situation

'Telling stories is far from unusual in everyday conversation and it is apparently no more unusual for interviewees to respond to questions with narratives if they are given some room to speak' (Mishler, 1986: 69). Indeed, in many cases, answers given in an interview are spontaneously formed into narratives. This is usually the case of interviews aiming at life histories or, in an organizational context, at career descriptions, where a narrative is explicitly asked for and delivered. This is also the case of interviews aiming at a historical description of a certain process, although the narrative may then be seen only as an introduction to the 'interview proper' that would switch to an analytical mode, aiming at producing logico-scientific knowledge. When the topic of an interview is a reform or a reorganization (that is, a chain of events that unfold in time), there is nothing unusual in formulating a question that prompts a narrative: 'Can you recall when you first started to talk about the necessity of reorganizing your department? And what happened next?'

But in most cases both sides have to combat the shared conviction that 'true knowledge' is not made of narratives. 'Why did you decide to reform?' and 'What were the factors that made a reorganization necessary?' will be perceived as more 'scientific' questions, prompting analytic answers. Also, the questions concerning 'the beginnings' are not as innocuous as they seem.

In what follows I quote two examples taken from my studies of big-city management where, in the first stage of the project, I conducted a round of interviews with the politicians and the officials managing the city, to be followed by shadowing (Czarniawska, 2002). The first example comes from Warsaw, the second from Stockholm; the first interlocutor was a woman and the second a man:

BC: Would you start with describing your work, please? What do you do?
      What are your responsibilities? How does your working day look?
I: No. Sorry, but in my case, I must begin with history.

This short example illustrates a type of difficulty often experienced by researchers interested in oral history. Paul Connerton pointed out that, while oral historians usually, and unreflectively, assume a chronological timing of an account, their interlocutors might have another time frame. People whose life is not controlled by modern institutions might see their life not as a 'curriculum vitae', a current of life, but as a series of cycles. The basic cycle is the day, then the week, the month, the season, the year, the generation (Connerton, 1989: 20).

Connerton makes an important point but he underestimates the amount of 'premodern' in modern institutions. Cyclical time is, in fact, a very obvious way of measuring time in contemporary organizations: workdays, workweeks, budget years, and generations. In the example above, it was I who suggested the cyclical timeframe ('a working day'), whereas my interlocutor chose to place her actions with reference to their place in the history of the social settings to which she belonged (Connerton, 1989: 21). The point is, the interviewees might choose diverse timeframes for their account: chronological, cyclical, or kairotic (a narrative time, punctuated by important events, which might even run backward in chronology).

It is important to let the interlocutors choose their own time frame. Asking 'when did it all begin?' is not especially helpful, as my earlier example indicated. In the present case, the interview in Warsaw was saved at the outset as my interlocutor took control of the interaction, much to my relief. I had no such luck in Stockholm, however:

BC: What do you see as the main task in your work?
I: My task is to fill the role of a group leader of the next-to-largest political party and to lead the opposition.
BC: But what does it mean in terms of your job? What do you do?
I: The political sciences state clearly that this role is that of a person who, in a democracy, was elected to be the foremost representative of some kind of a political movement or a group.
BC: But what kind of tasks do you perform? You come here every morning, and then, what do you do?
I: All that has to do with governance and management of the city.

We went on like that for a good while until I struck a lucky solution: I asked my interlocutor to describe his previous day in the office in detail. It resulted in the most minimalist kind of a narrative based on chronology only ('In the morning I met my party colleagues …'). But the very poverty of this narrative prompted elaboration: 'You must know that, at present, we are trying to develop a new way of working together' and a narrative ensued. Almost every fragmented detail of the day served as an element in a story of its own.

I am not quoting these excerpts simply to document my clumsiness as an interviewer, lamentable as it may be. Clever interviewers who never make mistakes reduce their interlocutors to puppets reciting what the researcher has previously thought up. As Latour (2000) points out, the true irony of the comparison between the natural and social scientists is that, while the former encounter a continuous resistance in their objects, who do not want to do what researchers tell them to, the social subjects eagerly play a role of pliable objects when asked to do so in the name of Science.

The apparent misunderstanding between me and the second interlocutor reveals, however, further interesting things about research interviews. I wanted to know what he did, but he told me what his role was, in abstract terms. One could say, borrowing Bourdieu's (1990) term, that I wished to reconstruct the logic of practice, but could one say that my interlocutor's answer followed the logic of theory? In part, yes; after all, he even quoted political science to legitimize his answer. But the logic dominating his response is what I called a logic of representation (Czarniawska, 1999b), and what Bourdieu called 'officialization' (1990).

I use 'representation' here in only one of its many meanings: not in the sense of rendering an equivalent of something else, as in 'representation theory of truth', and not in the sense of 'political representation', but in the sense of 'presenting oneself in a good light'. The logic of representation is like an elegant outfit put on when visitors are coming. It is used by everybody in positions that require official accounting for organizational practices. It borrows from the logic of practice its fondness for narratives but its narratives are stylized and abstract. They never take place in concrete circumstances but usually start with 'if' or 'imagine that'. It borrows from the logic of theory its models of formal rationality, where the carefully selected means lead to achievement of wisely chosen goals. It quotes from both practice and theory but, in contrast to both, it is rhetorically skillful and self-conscious.

It is mostly the logic of representation, the dressing up for visitors, which is exhibited during research interviews. But there is always an improvisation in an interview which is absent from formal representations such as annual reports and corporate videos. All interactions contain mixed styles of representation and quotations from different types of logic. A friend might quote a poem to better express his feelings or a colleague might relate during a coffee-break a whole theory she read the day before. Also, the logic of representation is but a more conscious and elaborate form of everyday accounts, an example of a correct grammar of motives (Burke, 1945). As Scott and Lyman observed in their influential article, '[a]n account is a linguistic device employed whenever an action is subjected to valuative inquiry' (1968: 46). Thus, it is the account type of narratives we want but do not always obtain.

Avoiding accounts

Scott and Lyman continue by explaining that accounts are made to explain 'unanticipated or untoward behavior' (1968), and this circumstance seems to indicate a difference between spontaneous accounts and research interviews. I would claim that, to the contrary, this caveat shows why the responses in research interviews are accounts in the exact sense of that given by Scott and Lyman: 'An account is not called for when people engage in routine, common-sense behavior in a cultural environment that recognizes that behavior as such' (1968: 47). When managers manage they engage in routine, commonsense behavior in a cultural environment that recognizes their behavior as such. A research interview is a staged situation where, by mutual consent, the recognition of a given behavior as 'routine and common sense' is suspended. The researchers play the role of 'foreigners' or 'visitors from another planet', whereas the practitioners agree to explain their behavior as if it were not routine and commonsensical, thus making it into 'action'.

Reconciled to the ubiquitous presence of the logic of representation (the logic of practice is present in interviews only insofar as they are the practice of taking part in an interview) and acknowledging the account-like character of interview responses, we might want to learn from Scott and Lyman about the usual strategies for avoiding accounts, as these are strategies that will exclude or impoverish narratives in an interview. They mention three: mystification, referral, and identity switching.

A *mystification* occurs when 'an actor admits that he is not meeting the expectations of another, but follows this by pointing out that, although there are reasons for his unexpected actions, he cannot tell the inquirer what they are' (1968: 58). In many studies, a mystification might have legal grounds, as when information is classified as confidential or when recounting somebody else's behavior can be read as slander. But it is the *referral* that is most commonly used: the interlocutor refers the researcher to a more competent source of information ('If you want to know what we do, look at the web') or refuses to speculate about other people's perceptions ('I am afraid you must ask her how she felt when this happened'). Another kind of referral is the one that happens in the interview I quoted above: my interlocutor referred me to political science, where a legitimate account of his activities was to be found. An *identity switching* (that is, pointing out that the researcher assumes another interlocutor's persona than the one he or she wishes to present) is also frequent: 'I am not a person who tells tales.' After all, to quote Scott and Lyman for the last time, 'every account is a manifestation of the underlying negotiation of identities' (1968: 59).

An interesting addition to this list comes from science studies (Mulkay and Gilbert, 1982). The scientists interviewed by the two authors did not account for, and thus did not produce narratives about, what they considered to be *correct knowledge.* They accounted for and told stories about errors and mistakes. This throws additional light on my difficulties reported above: confronted with 'correct knowledge', I could hardly question it or feign ignorance. An impasse occurred which could be resolved only by re-establishing the premises that made it legitimate for the interviewer to 'wonder'.

How, then, to obtain narratives in a situation which prompts the use of the logic of representation and offers many possibilities of avoiding an account? There are a great many suggestions, varying from the ways of eliciting stories (Mishler, 1986; Gabriel, 2000), through eliciting descriptive material (Spradley, 1979), to eliciting any type of response (Johnson and Weller, 2002). My problem with many of those suggestions is that they try to generalize and to abstract from situated experiences. I suggest that these texts be treated as a valuable collection of research narratives but I would warn, as before, against treating them as recipes. What worked miracles in one situation might cause trouble in another. It is important to elicit a narrative concerning the issue of interest to the researcher, but … sometimes another issue, brought spontaneously by the interviewee, turns out to be more interesting.

The discussion above reviews the difficulties of eliciting any kind of narrative at all. Once this difficulty has been overcome (skillfully or clumsily), the next concern is to get a complete story or a narrative. There, the commonsensical schemes suggested by Gabriel or Flanagan (as reported in Chapter 3) are as good as any. Personally, I recommend a 'recall check': will I be able to retell this story? If not, what is missing?

Interview transcript as a narrative

There are basically two things that can be done with – and to – narratives elicited in interviews. The first is to concoct a researcher's own *narrative out of them* – that is, to write up, or to rewrite, or to interpret them. These are synonyms – after all, each act of interpretive reading writes a story anew. Treated in this way, the narratives coming from interviews do not differ from other narratives: field notes, documents, official histories. The ways of reading and analyzing them will be reviewed in the remaining chapters.

The second is to analyze them as *narratives of interviews*, a special kind of texts. Conversation analysis offers technically sophisticated ways of dealing with such texts when they are taken to be inscriptions of social interactions. Here I suggest a way of looking at the *interview as an inscription of narrative production.*

The following radio interview has been recorded and transcribed by Veronica Gabrielli from Padua,[1] whom I thank for permission to use it. It was originally transcribed with the notation of conversation analysis, but my subsequent translation from Italian to English made this notation unusable. I have, however, preserved the capital letters for indicating the emphasis:

An interview with Isabella Spagnolo, grower of the red chicory of Treviso, and Sergio Grasso, both pioneers of 'safe foods'

1. *Paola, the journalist*: We are here in the kitchen to talk about the coming week that is very IMPORTANT to us. On Sunday, the 3rd of December, in 100 Italian cities will take place an event 'Friendly countryside', an exhibition aimed at TEACHING people about the most authentic produce in our country. We start with this VERY YOUNG producer, who is a role model for many women in the Northeast Italy. Let us move to the district of Treviso together with Isabella Spagnolo who is a GROWER of the RED CHICORY of Treviso. Good morning!

2. *Isabella*: Good morning Paola.

3. *Paola*: Good morning Isabella. Welcome. We have also with us another pioneer, even he from Treviso...

4. *Sergio*: Hmm, sort of a pioneer...

5. *Paola*: ... our Sergio Grasso. Well, when we say RED CHICORY ... let us begin with saying that you are so INCREDIBLY YOUNG, yet you threw yourself, soul and body, into this production...

6. *Isabella*: Yes, one may say so...

7. *Paola*: ... with passion.

8. *Isabella*: Exactly. I am ENTHUSIASTIC about agriculture, as I claim that at this moment it has a FUNDAMENTAL importance for us all. And exactly because we are the PIONEERS of safe foods, and we are CERTAIN of what we are producing and how we are producing it...

9. *Paola*: It is the slogan of our times...

10. *Isabella*: This product of ours, of the district of Treviso, is FABU-LOUS, it is a miracle of nature. It is not as you people see it in the field, because the miracle takes place under the water, in the springs that you can find ONLY in the district of Treviso, which cause that the heart of the chicory matures into this BEAUTIFUL red chicory...

11. *Paola*: This means that if I come for a visit to YOUR region, I won't see this in the fields...

12. *Isabella*: No, it is truly a MIRACLE, an EMOTION, which grows only in the earth where there are warm springs, so that chicory is collected from the FIELD, and put under the water, and thus this strange flower, called FLOWER OF THE WINTER, blooms.

13. *Paola*: As you could hear, Isabella is not only an enthusiast, she is also a poetess. We need to take a short break now, and afterwards you must tell me all....

14. *Paola*: This BEAUTIFUL, BEAUTIFUL woman of 29, Isabella Spagnolo, who is now sitting next to me, is a coordinator of women entrepreneurs associated in Coldiretti di Treviso... but also a producer of wine and...

15. *Isabella*: ... of red chicory.
16. *Paola*: ... of red chicory. And now we turn to our Sergio, who is from Treviso, to talk about red chicory, but the red chicory from Treviso. This goldmine that you have...
17. *Sergio*: This flower that we eat...
18. *Paola*: This flower that we eat...
19. *Sergio*: THAT from Treviso is called FLOWER THAT WE EAT, whereas that from Castelfranco, a stone's throw away from Treviso, is called the ROSE OF CASTELFRANCO. It is a chicory...
20. *Paola*: Now then, Isabella...
21. *Sergio*: ... and there are many chicories, but the one from Treviso is certainly the best whitened chicory, that is, submitted to the process of LIGHTENING, is the BEST chicory of all, belongs to the most innovative tradition, as it can be used in many ways.
22. *Paola*: Isabella, a young girl like you who is a producer, that is, who cultivates, what is your life like? That is, what is your work like?
23. *Isabella*: Certainly the most important is the MANAGEMENT of production, as we obviously feel the burden of the responsibility that we have, and this is the responsibility to GUARANTEE the quality of the product, in fact our product is marked IGP, a trademark that says that the product can be made only in the specific district, Treviso, OUR DISTRICT, and that is submitted to QUALITY control, thus we deliver a certified product and feel responsible for it. After which there is the COMMERCIAL part of it, the presentation of the product, like the one I am doing now, where we need to tell what we do... that for us it is the usual way...
24. *Paola*: Well, Isabella, how much PRIDE brings this product to Treviso, as it travels all around the world...
25. *Isabella*: It is an outer point of the diamond[2] formed by FABULOUS products from Veneto region such as potatoes, asparagus, beans, squash and wine, and many other products which go well with the red chicory of Treviso.
26. *Paola*: Well, how do you cook it?
27. *Isabella*: There is a LOT of ways. It is wonderful fried, grilled, fantastic for making *risotto con radicchio*, obviously you put LOTS of chicory and little rice, this is fundamental for this dish, and then you can combine it, it goes well with the wine from ITS land, Rabboso, which is born... it is a truly ABORIGINAL, you find it only in the province of Treviso, and then...
28. *Paola*: ABORIGINAL ... you are also aboriginal.
29. *Isabella*: ... well, yes... I am in love with nature and with the PRODUCT ...
30. *Paola*: And this is the end, Isabella Spagnolo will be in the city square on this Sunday dedicated to Coldiretti ...
31. *Isabella*: I will! there will be, on hundred squares, WE young producers from Coldiretti, and we will offer to the consumers the products with a certified QUALITY, so that the consumer will trust

us, trust that we do with such love, such passion and constant
dedication...

32. *Paola*: ... and she is only 29... Who knows where will she be in 10
years! Thank you Isabella Spagnolo, thank you Sergio Grasso, and
thank you, the red chicory of Treviso!

I chose this interview because, in my reading, it represents an interesting case
of a 'battle over a narrative' that is made distinct by the specific format of a
radio interview. A real-time interview is severely limited in time; the person
officially in power (the journalist) cannot use many of her privileges and has
to fight on an (almost) equal footing. In this sense, it is an exception from the
usual battle over a narrative but its exceptional character only serves to high-
light its character.

The battle is mostly fought between Paola and Isabella and it concerns the
protagonist of the narrative: is it to be a young woman entrepreneur or the red
chicory of Treviso? Paola opts for the first, Isabella opts for the second. Sergio
is on Isabella's side and therefore Paola has not much use for him: he is allowed
to speak once (utterances 17–21) but already at utterance 19 Paola wants to
return to Isabella as it is clear that Sergio will continue to speak of red chicory.
(We never learn what age he is.)

Paola seems to want to know all about Isabella, not about red chicory (she
even says so in utterance 13). Until the break, the narratives are on a par, as
Isabella speaks of red chicory whereas Paola punctuates the ways in which
Isabella speaks of red chicory, thus concentrating the attention on Isabella. After
the break, however, Isabella's narrative wins. Sergio supports it.

After Paula has taken the floor from Sergio, she attempts to elicit Isabella's
life story (or at least work life story) in utterance 22. But Isabella delivers a
eulogy of red chicory, framed in the fashionable terms of marketing (upon
checking, it has been confirmed that the young entrepreneurs associated in
Coldiretti were given marketing courses). By utterance 28 Paola gave up, the
time was coming to an end, and there was a slight touch of sarcasm audible on
the tape as she called Isabella 'also aboriginal'. At the end of the interview, she wit-
tingly recognized the true protagonist of the interview-born narrative, thank-
ing 'the red chicory of Treviso'.

My reading of this interview is supported by a fascinating study of Italian
women agricultural entrepreneurs conducted by Valérie Fournier (2002). She
showed how these women consciously used the identity of 'young women' or
withdrew from it for strategic purposes. Isabella is certainly a brilliant example
of this. Another interesting aspect of this interview is that Isabella is pushed into
an identity of 'young beautiful woman' not by a man but by another woman.
We all use conventional typifications of one another.

EXERCISE

Exercise 4.1: an interview as a site of narrative making

Record an interview from the radio or TV (an alternative: use a transcript of your own interview). Look for the traces of narratives-in-making: Can you see the work of emplotment? Are there competing narratives? Is the narrative-making successful?

FURTHER READING

Gubrium, Jaber F., and Holstein, J.A. (eds) (2002) *Handbook of Interview Research.* Thousand Oaks, CA: Sage.
Kvale, Steinar (1996) *InterViews. An Introduction to Qualitative Research Interviewing.* Thousand Oaks, CA: Sage.
Mishler, Elliot G. (1986) *Research Interviewing. Context and Narrative.* Cambridge, MA: Harvard University Press.
Riessman, Catherine Kohler (1993) *Narrative Analysis.* Newbury Park, CA: Sage.
Silverman, David (2001) *Interpreting Qualitative Data. Methods for Analysing Talk, Text and Interaction* (2nd edn). London: Sage.

Notes

1 As a part of coursework during a method course held by me at the University of Venice, Fall, 2000.
2 Isabella borrows this expression from Michael Porter, the guru of marketing.

5

Reading Narratives

Hernadi's triad

As there are a great many ways of reading (before one even decides whether it is an 'interpretation' or an 'analysis' that takes place), the 'hermeneutic triad' formulated by Paul Hernadi (1987) might be a helpful classificatory device. (see Table 5.1). It separates conceptually three ways of reading a text, in practice usually present simultaneously and intertwined. The attraction of his classification consists in, among other things, abolishing the traditional divides between 'interpretation' and 'explanation' by pointing out that various modes of reading are possible, and in fact desirable, at the same time. The triad begins with the simplest step – the rendering of a text in a reader's vocabulary ('what does this text say?'), continues with various ways of explaining it ('why does this text say what it does?' or 'how does this text say what it does?'), and ends with a step that is closer to writing than to reading: 'what do I, the reader, think of all this?'

Explication corresponds to a stance that the Italian semiotician, Umberto Eco (1990), calls that of *a naive* or *a semantic reader*. It is guided by an ambition to *understand* a text, and Hernadi uses here the famous literary theorist Northrop Frye's (1957) insight showing that it implies humility on the part of the reader: *standing under* the text. Explanation sets the reader above the text. The innocuous question 'what does the text say?' is replaced with an interruptive 'how does it say it?' (Silverman and Torode, 1980) or a more traditional 'why does the text say what it does?' This equals the stance of *a critical* or *a semiotic reader* (Eco, 1990). Hernadi's triad is egalitarian in that it puts all

TABLE 5.1   *The hermeneutic triad*

Explication	Explanation	Exploration
Standing under	Standing over	Standing in for
Reproductive translation	inferential detection	existential enactment
Reconstruction	Deconstruction	Construction

Source: After Hernadi (1987)

explanatory efforts on the same plane: be it semiotics, criticism, structural or rhetorical analysis, deconstruction – they all attempt to disassemble the text to see how it was made.

Exploration, or standing in for the author, might be seen as not appropriate for scientific texts, a genre that does not encourage existential enactment – that is, the readers bringing their lives and preoccupations into the text. Yet it can be found in most readings implicitly or explicitly: in the conclusion of a positivist scholar, in the confessional remarks of an ethnographer (Geertz, 1988; Van Maanen, 1988), in standpoint feminism (Smith, 1987; Martin, 1990; Calás and Smircich, 1991), and in empowerment ambitions of a narrative analyst (Mishler, 1986; Brown, 1998).

The difficulty of explication

While the most obvious way to explicate is to summarize somebody else's text (I will do this later), the issue of explication becomes much more complex when the narratives come from the field of practice under study. To begin with, they are many and they are rarely complete. Traditional rendering of this operation consists of the researcher writing 'the one true story' of what 'really happened' in a clear, authoritative voice. This procedure is nowadays considered an anathema, but such a judgment is somewhat hasty. After all, there are many good reasons to make up a consistent narrative out of many partly conflicting ones, or out of an incomplete or fragmented one; for instance, a coherent narrative is easy to read. The justice or injustice done to the original narrative depends on the attitude of the researcher and on the precautions he or she takes.

The second, and perhaps the main problem, is that of rendering somebody else's story in one's own idiom. No matter how well meaning the researcher is, such a translation is a political act of totalizing. This problem became acute in anthropology as literacy increased in previously oral societies (Lejeune, 1989). The Other, who before was just 'described', took on the task of self-description and of questioning the descriptions of the anthropologists. But when a field of practice under study is highly literate, the re-descriptions undertaken by the researchers are open to practitioners' comments and questions, which makes the problem less morally implicated but more politically complex. The status of science, especially the social sciences, does not stifle the protests and critiques any more. As I pointed out at some length in a different context (Czarniawska, 1998), the 'voices of the field' reported in organization studies are as literate and eloquent as those of the reporters, and often have greater political clout. Thus, the choice seems to lie between the Scylla of silencing other people and the Charybdis of trying to shout louder than they do.[1]

Whichever way is chosen, it does not release the researchers from the responsibility for what they write and the duty to respect their interlocutors. But this responsibility and respect do not have to be expressed in a literal repetition of what has been said. A researcher has a right, but also a professional duty, to do a 'novel reading', in an apt expression coined by Marjorie DeVault (1990): an interpretation by a person who is not socialized into the same system of meaning as the narrator but is familiar enough with it to recognize it as such. At any given time and place, she continues, there are *dominant and marginal readings* of the same text and, I may add, there are a number of narratives reporting the same developments but plotting them in different ways, as we have seen in the examples of studies by Gabriel (2000) and Sköldberg (2002). Some plots are dominant while others are considered marginal, but it is not necessary that the researcher subscribe to the dominant plot. Agreement is not always the best way of expressing respect. The researchers' duty is, however, to assume authorial responsibility for the narrative they concocted and also to admit the existence of opposition from the interlocutors, if they are aware of it.

There are many ways of paying respect to one's interlocutors. One is a multivoiced story, recommended by many anthropologists (see, e.g., Marcus, 1992). There are then not one but many narratives; as in a postmodern novel, all tell their story and the researcher does not have to take a stand on which is 'right' and which is 'wrong'. Thus Gabriel was able to quote all four accounts of an explosion of a fire extinguisher. One account was a chronicle that merely reported the sequence of events, while the remaining three constructed three different stories with different heroes, victims, and plots.

An excellent example of such a multistory is a novel by Iain Pears, *An Instance of the Fingerpost* (1998). It is a kind of a history of a medical invention (the transfusion) and is situated in seventeenth-century Oxford. It contains four stories accounting for the same course of events. The readers can choose which one to believe but the final effect is rather that of understanding why the stories differ as they do.

One has to point out, however, that polyphony in a text is but a textual strategy (Czarniawska, 1999a). 'The voices of the field' do not speak for themselves; it is the author who makes them communicate on his or her conditions. Therefore it is more adequate to speak, in line with Bakhtin (1928/1985), about 'variegated speech' of the field, about leaving traces of different dialects, different idioms, and different vocabularies, rather than homogenizing them into a 'scientific text'. This is actually Pears' most impressive achievement. Again, this textual strategy is not as drastically different from one authoritative story as it may seem. Even pasting together fragments of narratives taken straight from an interview protocol decontextualizes them but, in return, it also re-contextualizes them (Rorty, 1991). It is not a matter of 'quoting literally'; it is a matter of recontextualization that is interesting ('novel'), credible, and respectful. It is clear, however, that explication already prepares the ground for explanation and exploration.

Varieties of explanation

Explanation is often set in contrast to interpretation, but most likely Hernadi chose the word to achieve the alliteration effect. It can be argued, though, that certain types of hermeneutic thoughts advise a jump from explication to exploration. From the pragmatist point of view, however, such a jump is impossible as all explication is tinted with explanation and all inquiry asks both 'what does this text say?' and 'how come?' Similarly, hermeneutics, the philosophy and theory of interpretation, offered many a different suggestion on how to tackle interpretation in many ages of its existence. The point is that the question 'how come' assumes many guises in various schools of thought. Solutions change, but problems remain. As Umberto Eco put it:

> To interpret means to react to the text of the world or to the world of a text by producing other texts ... The problem is not to challenge the old idea that the world is a text which can be interpreted, but rather to decide whether it has a fixed meaning, many possible meanings, or none at all. (1990: 23)

Let me introduce a simple classification of different schools of thought concerning the modes of explanation, or interpretation, ordered into three groups: subjectivist (voluntarist), objectivist (determinist), and constructivist.

Subjectivist explanation: intentio auctoris or intentio lectoris?

Perhaps the most traditional way of explaining texts is by deducing the intentions of their author. This tradition comes from reading the Bible, Talmud or Koran as authored by God, and therefore the utmost task of the reader (an expert reader in Catholicism and Judaism, everybody in Protestantism and Islam) is to try to discover God's intentions.

Even so, there have been many opinions as how to proceed when trying to discover God's intentions. *Encyclopaedia Britannica* (1989, 5: 874) lists four major types of biblical hermeneutics. The first, *literal*, prohibited any kind of explanation: explication was the only operation permitted on the divine text. The second is *moral* hermeneutics, which seeks ethical lessons in the Bible. The third is *allegorical* interpretation, which assumes a second level of reference behind persons, things, and events explicitly mentioned in the Bible. The fourth type is called *anagogical*[2] or *mystical* and assumes that the Bible prefigures the future, the events to come. An excellent, if ironic, exemplification of this last kind of reading is to be found in Eco's *Foucault's Pendulum* (1989) quoted in the previous chapter, in which a group of Cabbalists discovers divine plots in all texts they come across.

Is biblical hermeneutics of any relevance for social science, apart from being a piece of historical information? Perhaps not literal and mystical, but moral and allegorical interpretations clearly are. They cannot be used in relation to narratives in the making – bits of interviews, conversations, observations – but they can be used whenever one can, in fact, speak of an author's intentions, as in advertisements or in various types of representation documents (annual reports, home pages, autobiographies). What is more, contemporary authors are themselves hermeneutic readers, quite often quoting the Bible when in search of ethical lessons and/or allegories that make sense to a contemporary reader.

In modern versions of hermeneutics, the divine author was replaced by the psyche of the human author. Such a move is attributed to Friedrich E.D. Schleiermacher (1768–1834), considered the founder of modern Protestant theology, who, through his interest in the classics and the Romantics, led away from the exegesis of the gospel toward a religion based on human culture (Robinson, 1995). He postulated that to gain the meaning of a text one has to understand the mind of the author because it is there where God lives and works. Phenomenology and psychoanalysis freed themselves from religious contexts but still read texts as traces of the state of mind of their author (Marcel Proust and James Joyce were perhaps the authors most frequently and thoroughly read this way).

Looking for an author's intention was never a distinct tradition in the reading of scientific texts (in other sense than pure explication or 'what the author intended to say'). This was because the author's psyche was not supposed to interfere with the writing of a scientific text: the truth should be writing itself. But the subjectivist approach was, and still is, applied to 'subjects' – people under study and the narratives produced by them.

In literary theory and philosophy, the most potent response to the tradition of *intentio auctoris* was Gadamer's hermeneutics (1960/1975). This book is not the right place to give justice to his work that, as a blurb on *Truth and Method* correctly says, 'takes the literature of Hermeneutics to new heights'. For Gadamer, hermeneutics was a philosophy, a quest for truth, and only marginally a method (indeed, Ricoeur, 1981, claims that Gadamer's book should have had the title 'Truth OR Method'). Gadamer himself says of his work that '[i]t is concerned to seek that experience of truth that transcends the sphere of control of scientific method wherever it is to be found, and to inquire into its legitimacy' (1960/1975: xii). Human sciences should join philosophy, art, and history: 'modes of experience in which a truth is communicated that cannot be verified by the methodological means proper to science' (p. xii). At the same time, Gadamer claims he does not intend to continue Dilthey's distinction between the 'human' and the 'natural' sciences and their methods. He is not against applying natural sciences' methods to the social world, but such an endeavor has nothing to do with reaching truth through experience; it belongs with practicalities and bureaucracy. Similarly, he claims to have gone beyond Romanticism and subjectivism, but his critics show that all these influences are still decisive in Gadamer's work. This critique is understandable in the light of the following statement: 'Understanding must be conceived as a part of the process of the coming into being of meaning, in which the significance of all statements ... is formed and made complete' (Gadamer, 1960/1975: 146).

The possibility of meaning which will reveal the significance of all statements is an ultimate Romantic dream; also, even a small portion of inter-subjectivity will put into question and on to the table of argumentation the judgment of 'completeness'. But my comments are not an attempt to diminish a brilliant contribution of a great philosopher; they are only a way to point out that, in spite of Gadamer's protestation, the attraction of his version of hermeneutics is its Romanticism, subjectivism, and his mistrust of natural science methods applied to humanities. In his view, such methods assume and require an *alienating distanciation* as opposed to the *experience of belonging* typical in arts, history, and humanities. It will take Ricoeur to point out the possibility of joining the two. And if Gadamer still remains close to subjectivity, it is the subjectivity of the reader, not of the author; it is the reader's experience that leads to truth as understanding. What is more, this experience is verified by tradition in a kind of temporal intersubjectivity. In this way, the road to reader-response theory has been paved. Similarly, Gadamer's observation of language's formative influence on thought makes room for both objectivist and constructivist theories of reading.

Objectivist explanations

Objectivist explanations are the proper territory of sciences, and literary theory experienced a period of scientification, especially in the 1970s, when sociology was at its peak. One kind of objectivist explanation is by relation to external structures: class, power relationships, gender, or even a specific historical situation. Even if the writers' biographies might count, the authors are seen as 'children of their times' and their texts, accordingly, as 'products of their times'. Marxist, neo- and post-Marxist works are examples of such a kind of explanation.

Jürgen Habermas's work has been of enormous importance for the social sciences. His focus is not so much hermeneutics as critique of ideology which, however, can also count as a theory of reading. His relationship to Marxism, points out Ricoeur (1981), is like Gadamer's to Romantic philosophy: distancing and yet belonging. The task of critical social sciences – and therefore of critical reading – is to unmask interests that underlie the enterprise of knowledge (Habermas, 1972). This task differentiates critical social sciences from both empirical-analytical studies of social order and from historical-hermeneutic studies suggested by Dilthey and Gadamer. The purpose of the critical social sciences is emancipation, which is achieved by self-reflection. The critical social sciences provide the tool for such emancipation, revealing the relations of dependence hidden behind relations (not forces, as in Marxism) of production. Self-reflection prompted by critical social science is the road to freedom from institutions.

Another variation of the Marxist theory of interpretation can be found in the literary theory of, for example, Fredric Jameson (Jameson, 1981; Selden, 1985). He calls it a 'dialectical criticism', as it strongly focuses on the Hegelian notion of the relationship between the part and the whole (the idea behind all conceptualizations of 'hermeneutic circle'[3]), the concrete and the abstract, the subject and the object, the dialectics of appearance and essence. This kind of criticism does not analyze isolated works; each work is but a part of a wider historical situation, and so is each reading. A dialectical criticism seeks to unmask the surface of the text to reach the depth of the concrete historical ideology that informed it. While Habermas is mostly concerned with the notion of 'dialogue', Jameson is strongly convinced about the central role of narrative in human knowledge: the narrative is a basic 'epistemological category' to be met everywhere and which needs to be interpreted.

Jameson's dialectical criticism is close to another kind of objectivist explanation: structuralism. Indeed, his treatment of narratives recalls that of Barthes, and he uses Greimas' categories in analysis. This is hardly surprising: Selden (1985) points out that the economic writings of Karl Marx are structuralist. But as structuralism and deconstruction are not only 'philosophies of reading' but also techniques, they will be treated in subsequent chapters.

A third example of a post-Marxist theory of reading is the one from a feminist standpoint, best represented by Dorothy Smith (1990; 1999). Her readings are aimed at exploring the *relations of ruling*:

> The institutional order of the society that excluded and silenced women and women's experience is elucidated from women's standpoint in the local actualities of our everyday/everynight world as they are organized extra-locally, abstracted, grounded in universalized forms, and objectified. The phrase 'relations of ruling' designates the complex of extra-local relations that provide in contemporary societies a specialization of organization, control and initiative. They are those forms that we know as bureaucracy, administration, management, professional organization, and the media. They include also the complex of discourses, scientific, technical, and cultural, that intersect, interpenetrate, and coordinate the multiple sites of ruling. (1990: 6)

In an essay 'K is mentally ill' (1990), Smith analyzes an interview showing how K comes to be defined by her friends as mentally ill.[4] In 'The social organization of subjectivity' (1990) she analyzes a transcript of a meeting at the University of British Columbia in the 'hot year' of 1969. In 'The active text' (1990) she compares two texts describing the same course of events: a confrontation between police and people in Berkeley, California, in the 1960s. One is a letter published in an underground newspaper and the other is a leaflet with the Mayor of Berkeley's version of the events.

A point worth emphasizing is that the work of Dorothy Smith could be as well classified under 'constructivist' explanations. Using inspiration from Schütz and ethnomethodology, she highlights the relations of ruling as processes, not as structures. The key word is 'objectified' rather than 'objective'. This shows, once again, that the differences between various perspectives are very subtle, although they sometimes become exaggerated for the sake of enacting 'paradigm wars'. But the authors presented throughout this book have one thing in common: their interest in, and their conviction of the importance of, narratives. Rather than wasting time and energy on fighting battles with other schools of thought, they learn from each other.

Constructivist explanations

The theoreticians I am discussing below are not usually referred to as 'constructionist', and it is not my intention to justify such labeling of their work. I have chosen to present it under this title because what they all have in common is a belief that the meaning of a text is neither to be 'found' nor 'created' from nothing: it is *constructed* anew from what already exists (a text, a tradition, a genre) in the interaction between the readers and the text, among the readers, and between the author, the readers, and the text.

One kind of constructivist explanation is known as *reader-response* theory. German literary theorist, Wolfgang Iser, and aesthetic theorist, Hans Robert Jauss, have both extended and criticized Gadamer's work and created their own reception theory, where especially Iser emphasizes the interaction between the reader and the text (1978). Reader-response theory continues the phenomenological inspiration, but is also influenced by US pragmatism in the rendition of William James (while Umberto Eco and Richard Rorty, see below, are influenced by, respectively, Charles Peirce and John Dewey). For Iser:

> a meaning must clearly be the product of an interaction between the textual signals and the reader's acts of comprehension … As text and reader thus merge into a single situation, the division between subject and object no longer applies, and therefore follows that *meaning* is no longer an object to be defined, but *is an effect to be experienced*. (1978: 10, emphasis added)

And if meaning is an effect produced (or not) in an encounter between the reader and the text, 'the interpreter should perhaps pay more attention to the process than to the product' (1978: 18). The meaning production becomes more interesting than *the* meaning; this alone puts literary theory closer to social science.

But if meaning equals experience, all the criticisms directed at Gadamer's hidden subjectivism might apply. Iser concedes that a subjectivist element might come in at a late stage of interpretation, where the effect restructures experience – in other words, in the stage of exploration. At the stage of explanation, however, the reader follows 'intersubjectively verifiable instructions for meaning-production' that each text contains, even if it may end in a variety of experiences (Iser, 1978: 25). This notion makes Iser's ideas close to Eco's *intentio operis*; indeed, Eco borrows Iser's concept of an 'implied reader'.

The pragmatists, however, are not in agreement over what a *pragmatist* theory of reading should be. In response to the recent wave of polysemous theories of interpretation that claim that readings are countless, Eco (1992) pointed out that interpretations are indefinite but not infinite. They are negotiations between the intention of the reader (*intentio lectoris*) and the intention of the text (*intentio operis*). These negotiations can result in a first-level reading (typical for a semantic reader) or an overinterpretation, a reading that ignores the text (a tendency of a semiotic reader). Most readers live some place between those two extremes, and different readers have different interpretation habits.

Richard Rorty (1992) had difficulty in accepting Eco's pragmatic interpretation model precisely because of his pragmatist position. Despite all repudiations, there is a clear hierarchy between Eco's two extreme readers: the semiotic reader is a clever one (presumably a researcher), whereas the semantic reader is a dupe (presumably an unreflective practitioner). Also, the difference proposed by Eco between an 'interpretation' (which respects *intentio operis*) and 'use' (for example, lighting a fire with a text, but more generally just a disrespectful reading) is something that Rorty could not accept. For him, all readings are 'uses'. If a classification of uses – i.e. readings – is required, Rorty suggested a distinction between a *methodical reading*, one that is controlled by the reader and the purpose at hand, and an *inspired reading*, which changes the reader and the purpose as much as it changes the text.

So, who is right? At this point other constructionist theories of interpretation might be of help. What is a 'reasonable interpretation' and what is an 'overinterpretation' is negotiated not so much between the text and the reader as among the readers (intersubjectivity). In that sense, *intentio operis* is but a frequent reading of a given text in a given place at a given time. It is impossible, however, to establish the *intentio operis* of a given text once and for all. Intentions are being read into the text each time a reader interprets it. Again, this does not mean there is an unlimited variety of an idiosyncratic interpretation. If genres are institutionalized ways of writing, there are also institutionalized ways of reading, such as 'new criticism' or 'deconstruction'. In a given time and place there will be dominant and marginal readings of the same text (DeVault, 1990), and this makes the notion of 'interpretive communities' very useful (Fish, 1989). Social science still lacks efforts to discover and describe such interpretive communities of its own readers.

Of relevance here are *institutionalist* explanations that look for inspiration in genre theory, which is a literary theory of institutions. A genre is usually conceived as a system of action which became institutionalized and is recognizable by repetition; its meaning stems from its place within symbolic systems making up literature and culture, acquiring specificity by difference from other genres (Bruss, 1976: 5). A genre offers to a writer a repertoire of expressive means and to a reader a repertoire of reading clues. Although the writers might subvert and transgress genres, and so may the readers, they can both rely on this recognizable repertoire. When we recognize a text as a detective story, we form certain expectations about how it should proceed; if it does not, it might enchant us (a new genre is emerging!) or disappoint us (this is a bad detective story).

Although I myself opt for constructionist explanations, there are a great many excellent explanations of subjectivist and objectivist type. One can ask: what are the reasons (motives) behind this text? Which are the causes that formed this text? How is this text read and by whom? Or how does this text say what it does? All are excellent questions and they all have in common one thing: they interrogate a text, which is the *raison d'être* of each inquiry. One way of doing so seems especially suitable for social sciences and therefore I present it separately here: it is an analogy between an action and a text, postulated by Paul Ricoeur.

Action as text; text as action

The French philosopher, Paul Ricoeur, while essentially operating from within the reader-oriented end of the spectrum, was uncomfortable with the intrinsic subjectivity associated with such hermeneutics and decided to walk the fine line between a call for objectivity (grounded in the text) and the possibility of a great many interpretations of the same text (Robinson, 1995). He both integrated and went beyond the works of Gadamer and Habermas.

In order to be able to do this, he introduced a specific understanding of a text (a written narrative). To him, the text is primarily a work of *discourse* – that is, a structured entity that cannot be reduced to a sum of sentences that create it. This entity is structured according to rules that permit its recognition of belonging to some kind of a literary *genre*: a novel, a dissertation, a play. Even if each text can be classified as belonging to some genre (or as transgressing some genre), it has its unique *composition*, and when such composition is repeated in the work of the same author, one can speak of a *style*. Composition, genre, and style reveal the work that was put into creating a given specimen of discourse.

But it is important to notice that the text is a *written* work of discourse, which means that it is more than the inscription of an earlier speech (this is why such inscriptions cannot be read and analyzed in the same way as proper texts). Speaking and writing are two separate modes of discourse. Ricoeur (1981; John B. Thompson, 1981) introduced the concept of *distanciation* to point out the difference between the two. Text has acquired a distance from speech (even if it might have been originated in a speech). This statement is of no surprise to anyone who has tried to turn an oral presentation into a paper.

The first form of distanciation consists in that – through a text – meaning acquires a longer life than just the event of the speech. The institution of minutes corroborates this.

The second form of distanciation concerns the intentions of the speaker and the inscribed speech. While, in the case of speech, looking for *intentio auctoris* makes sense, as the speaker can always deny having said a concrete thing, when it comes to interpretation of the text, the author and the reader acquire more or less equal status. This is, by the way, why sending the transcripts of the interview to the interviewees is a risky procedure: the interviewee considers the transcript of the interview a written text and corrects it accordingly. The corrected text has little to do with the original speech, not because the interviewer heard wrongly but because the two are different forms of discourse.

The third form of distanciation concerns the distance between the two audiences: a speech is addressed to a concrete audience (even in the case of radio and TV speeches, where there are statistics showing who listens to what and when), while a written text is potentially addressed to anyone who can read. A (common) conviction that texts can be written for a concrete audience is based either on the belief in the repetition of the past (the past readers of John Grisham's novels will most likely be the readers of John Grisham's future novels), or on the belief in the possibility of creating the text's own audience, of shaping the reader, as Flaubert said of Balzac. In authors who are neither Grishams nor Balzacs, such a conviction is an expression of either naïveté or hubris.

The fourth form of distanciation concerns the text's separation from the frame of reference the speaker and the audience might have shared, or might have created together. During a talk, it is enough to ask the audience whether they are familiar with a certain segment of reality and adapt the speech accordingly. The frame of reference of future readers remains unknown to the writer. 'Will they be old enough to remember who Gerard Philippe was?'[5] is a kind of question that cannot be answered with certainty in advance. Texts intended for a certain audience can be unexpectedly adopted by quite another type of audience. William Gibson, author of science fiction novels, was surprised to learn that computer programmers become inspired by his books (Kartvedt, 1994/95).

This way of defining the text has consequences for the theory of interpretation. The two first forms of distanciation mean that 'the problem of the right understanding can no longer be solved by a simple return to the alleged intentions of the author' (Ricoeur, 1981: 211). The other two forms of distanciation, the unknown audience and its unknown frame of reference, can be dealt with in two different ways. One is the structuralists' (and poststructuralists') way: concentrate on the text alone, leaving aside the question of its possible referents. The second is the one proffered by Ricoeur himself: 'to situate explanation and interpretation along a unique *hermeneutical arc* and to integrate the opposed attitudes of explanation and understanding within an overall conception of reading' (1981: 161). The analogy between the text and the action, which I mentioned in Chapter 1 as one way of introducing narrative to social sciences, is an example of such a conception of reading.

Meaningful action shares the constitutive features of the text: it becomes objectified by inscription, which liberates it from its agent; it has relevance beyond its immediate context; and it can be read like an 'open work'. Similarly, a text can be attributed to an agent (the author); it is possible to ascribe (rather than 'establish') intentions to its author; and it has consequences, often unexpected. In such conceptualization, a text does not 'stand for' an action; the relationship between them is that of an analogy, not a reference.

Exploration

Exploration means the reader stands in for the author, becomes the author. This may be unusual with most readers but it is the meaning of the practice of social science. The social science reader reads in order to become an author: no matter what school of explication and explanation he or she belongs to, no matter whether the reading turns out to be methodical or inspired in kind. This is why Chapters 8 and 9 are dedicated to modes of writing as the final act in scientific reading.

The modes of exploration will differ according to the theory of reading espoused. The subjectivists, as mentioned before, might skip explanation and reveal their own experience as the way of exploring the topic. The objectivists might skip the exploration, or rather treat the combination of an explication and an explanation as producing the exploration: a recounting of a text combined with a text's critique amounts to an 'improved' text. The constructivists might want to spend some time on reflection over their own process of interpretation or they might not; they may also skip explanation and use explication as a building material for their own stance.

One case of an amazing exploration is, however, worth mentioning. This is Donna Haraway's 'A cyborg manifesto' (1991). It can perhaps be compared to Thomas Nagel's 'What is it like to be a bat?'[6] (1979). But while Nagel designed a gentle philosophical thought experiment, Haraway is literal:

> By the late 20th century, we are all chimeras, mythic hybrids of machine and organism, in short, cyborgs. In recent Western science and politics, the relation between organism and machine has been a border war. This essay is an argument for pleasure in the confusion of boundaries and for responsibility in their construction. A socialist-feminist must pay particular attention to the redesign of cyborgs, i.e. to genetic engineering. (1991: 149)

In this sense, all feminist writings are a huge exploration experiment: the non-gendered Author has been transformed into a woman, into a feminist, who looks at the world anew from the feminist standpoint. But Haraway goes even further and finds the 'female identity' a thing of the past. Her exploration is directed toward the future: people are cyborgs already and they are busy with further redesign of cyborgs (Haraway's later project concerns a genetically engineered mouse – 1997). What is it to be a cyborg?

> A cyborg body is not innocent; it was not born in a garden; it does not seek unitary identity and so generate antagonistic dualisms without end (or until the world ends); it takes irony for granted. One is too few, and two is only one possibility. Intense pleasure in skill, machine skill, ceases to be a sin, but an aspect of embodiment. The machine is not an it to be animated, worshipped, and dominated. The machine is us, our processes, an aspect of our embodiments ... Gender might not be the global identity after all. (Haraway, 1991: 179)

This is, then, a quintessence of exploration: to throw one's identity into a text or to construct one's identity through a text. Such a move is still rare in social sciences but it does not surprise anymore.

The short descriptions of various schools of reading that form this chapter do not permit their application to a concrete text, not only because they are brief and summary but also because they are philosophies, not methods or techniques, of reading. They are presented here because a choice of a method or technique of analysis needs to be preceded by a choice of a theory of reading that one finds agreeable. This book is therefore meant as an introduction to the repertoire of theories: the reader might then proceed to gather a more thorough knowledge of a theory that suits him or her.

I end this chapter with a short example of three phases in reading as a way of illustrating why such a reflection over which theory of reading to espouse is unavoidable.

Reading Egon Bittner

The following is a short excerpt from the classic text by Egon Bittner, 'The concept of organization' (1965):

3. The Study of the Concept of Organization as a Common-Sense Construct

> Plucked from its native ground, i.e. the world of common sense, the concept of rational organization, and the schematic determinations that are subsumed under it, are devoid of information on how its terms relate to facts. Without knowing the structure of this relationship of reference, the meaning of the concept and its terms cannot be determined.
>
> In this situation an investigator may use one of the three research procedures. He can, for one thing, proceed to investigate formal organization while assuming that the unexplicated common-sense meanings of the terms are adequate definitions for the

purposes of his investigation. In this case, he must use that which he proposes to study as a resource for studying it.

He can, in the second instance, attach to the terms a more or less arbitrary meaning by defining them operationally. In this case, the relationship of reference between the term and the facts to which it refers will be defined by the operations of inquiry. Interest in the actor's perspective is either deliberately abandoned, or some fictitious version of it is adopted.

The investigator can, in the last instance, decide that the meaning of the concept, and of all the terms and determinations that are subsumed under it, must be discovered by studying their use in real scenes of action by persons whose competence to use them is socially sanctioned. (p. 247)

Explication *(what does this text say?)*

Bittner lists three possible approaches to studying formal organizations. The first approach consists in assuming that people understand the concept 'formal organization' in the same way that the researcher does and in studying what he considers a formal organization to be. The second starts with the researcher introducing his own definition and proceeding accordingly, with no reference to other people's understanding. In the third, the researcher tries to discover how the concept is applied by people who use it to structure their own action.

I hope that this simple example shows how complex the operation of explication actually is. The text is shorter then Bittner's, but does it say the same thing? I had many a quarrel with students who understood it differently. Also, many times the sheer translation from one language to another (as when my students explicate it in Swedish or in Italian) changes the context of use: shall one translate literally? Or functionally? That is, looking for similar but not exactly the same expressions in the other language (volumes have been written about it; for the latest one, see Eco, 2003)? Also, observe the change of vocabulary: 'persons whose competence to use them is socially sanctioned' are 'competent members' – this is ethnomethodology speaking; 'people who use it to structure [the meaning of] their own action' is Wittgensteinian, or pragmatist. Thus an innocent explication is already halfway to explanation and exploration. I will follow this lead.

Explanation 1 *(why does this text say what it says?)*

It is easy to see that Bittner is writing it in 1965. The ethnomethodological revolution is in the offing (Garfinkel, Sacks, and Bittner himself) and their main enemy is positivism. Schützian phenomenology is a support, partly a starting point: concepts removed from the context of common sense lose their meaning but concepts that remain within the context of common sense cannot be explored. Thus, the first researcher is a dupe, a person who does not understand what the inquiry is all about. Probably, it is just a straw man to detract attention from the real target of attack. The second researcher is the positivist who does not care about the world of common sense: he just defines the word as it fits him and continues to study this 'figment of his imagination' [a typical expression used in those times in sociological debates]. The third researcher is a good guy; he is an ethnomethodologist.

Explanation 2 *(how does this text say what it says?)*

To the reader, this text might appear heavy handed and convoluted. Why, the subject of the first sentence consists of four clauses, enough to discourage the bravest of readers. But this apparent lack of style (or at least stylishness) might actually be a sign of style. Bittner's text is a contemporary of James D. Thompson's Organizations in Action *(1967), which I have quoted as exemplary of the 'scientistic' style so prevalent in the 1960s and the 1970s (Czarniawska, 1999a). It could even be that the heavy syntax is a remaining trace of the influence of German philosophy on US social science writing. Observe also the taken-for-granted use of the masculine pronoun.*

Kinds of explanation can be multiplied almost infinitely; they can also be combined, depending on the purpose of the reader. In fact, all kinds of text analysis presented in Chapters 6 and 7 can be applied to Bittner's text. What they all have in common, and so do my two 'explanations', is that they set the text against other texts, they 'contextualize' it (even deconstruction does it).

Exploration

Writing 35 years after Bittner, it seems obvious to me that the third strategy is the only one that makes sense. I know from my bitter experience of studies in different cultures that people whose practice I study very often use the same concepts in a way opposite to the way I do. But Bittner did not foresee one consequence of the second research stance: that the 'competent members' will become familiar with uses suggested by the second type of researcher and will hurl them at the third type of researcher. Often times, the researcher only reaps what her colleagues have sown before her.

The last comment and its agricultural metaphors are meant to be an allusion to the 'red chicory interview': there, the young entrepreneur used, in an everyday situation, textbook concepts to give meaning to her own experience. Not even everyday life and social science can be safely separated: social science feeds forward its own reading.

EXERCISE

Exercise 5.1: explication, explanation, exploration

Take a short text (which would qualify as a text by Ricoeur's definition) of one of your favorite social science writers and go through three reading phases.

FURTHER READING

Eco, Umberto (1992) *Interpretation and Overinterpretation.* Cambridge: Cambridge University Press.
Gadamer, Hans-Georg (1960/1975) *Truth and Method.* New York, NY: Continuum.
Iser, Wolfgang (1978) *The Act of Reading. A Theory of Aesthetic Response.* Baltimore, MD: Johns Hopkins University Press.
Jameson, Fredric (1981) *The Political Unconscious: Narrative as a Socially Symbolic Act.* Ithaca, NY: Cornell University Press.
Ricoeur, Paul (1981) *Hermeneutics and the Human Sciences.* New York, NY: Cambridge University Press.
Smith, Dorothy E. (1990) *Texts, Facts, and Femininity: Exploring the Relations of Ruling.* London: Routledge.

Notes

1 Scylla and Charybdis were, in Greek mythology, two monsters situated on both sides of the narrow waterway that Odysseus had to pass.
2 From the Greek *anagein* ('to refer').
3 A term often used by continental philosophers in the tradition running from Schleiermacher and Dilthey to Heidegger, Gadamer, and Ricoeur. It has to do with the inherent circularity of all understanding. The concept postulates that the unknown can be apprehended only by a mediation of that which is already known.
4 This is an analysis of an interview, which is exemplary both in how the account is elicited (issues discussed in Chapter 4) and the creative, non-formalist use of structural analysis (Chapter 6).
5 Tragically deceased French film-actor (1922–59), the icon of the 1950s.
6 Nagel received an energetic answer based on bat studies from Kathleen Akins (1993 – 'What is it like to be boring and myopic?').

6

Structural Analyses

One traditional way of analyzing a narrative is structuralist analysis – an enterprise close to semiology and formalism (Propp, 1928/1968; de Saussure, 1933/1983; Barthes, 1977). This enterprise was taken up and developed in anthropology by Claude Lévi-Strauss (1968). The socio-linguists William Labov and Joshua Waletzky espoused and improved on Propp's formalist analysis, suggesting that socio-linguistics should occupy itself with a syntagmatic analysis of simple narratives, which will eventually provide a key to understanding of the structure and functions of complex narratives. Their appeal has been taken up by several sociologists (Watson, 1973; Mishler, 1986; Riessman, 1993).

The morphology of a fairytale

Vladimir Propp (1895–1970) was a member of the Russian formalist group who wrote his *Morphology of the Folktale* in 1928, when the formalist trend ran into a crisis in the Soviet Union. Mikhail Bakhtin and his collaborators then developed what can be called a postformalism, under the guise of Marxist critique. But Propp's book is a classic example of structuralist analysis – applied to a collection of fairytales with the aim of describing Slavic folktales. His book was translated into English only in 1968, after Lévi-Strauss made it famous by his analysis of myths.

Propp's aim was highly scientific: he wished to classify forms of Slavic fairytales 'according to their component parts and the relationship of these components to each other and to the whole' (1968: 19): a morphology, as in botany. Having analyzed 100 fairytales (out of a collection of 449) he noticed that the same character can perform different actions and that different characters may perform the same action. Some actions can have different meanings depending on when and where in the narrative they take place, while others always have the same meaning. On this basis, Propp decided that the most important component of the tale is the function that an action of a character plays in the whole of the story. Consequently, he distilled a list of functions where *function* was understood as 'an act of a character, defined from the point of view of its significance for the course of action' (1968: 21).[1] I will quote this list of functions (together with their definitions) but without the formal notation (which, in my view, mystifies rather than clarifies the analysis; Propp abandoned it later[2]). These are as follows:

1 One of the members of a family absents himself from home. (ABSENTATION)
2 An interdiction is addressed to the hero. (INTERDICTION)
3 The interdiction is violated. (VIOLATION)
4 The villain makes an attempt at reconnaissance. (RECONNAISSANCE)
5 The villain receives information about his victim. (DELIVERY)
6 The villain attempts to deceive his victim in order to take possession of him or of his belongings. (TRICKERY)
7 The victim submits to deception and thereby unwittingly helps his enemy. (COMPLICITY)
8 The villain causes harm or injury to a member of a family. (VILLAINY)
8a One member of a family either lacks something or desires to have something. (LACK). [*At this point Propp breaks down and admits the difficulties of a disjoint classification.*]
9 Misfortune or lack is made known; the hero is approached with a request or command; he is allowed to go or he is dispatched. (MEDIATION, THE CONNECTIVE INCIDENT)
10 The seeker agrees to or decides upon counteraction. (BEGINNING COUNTERACTION)
11 The hero leaves home. (DEPARTURE)
12 The hero is tested, interrogated, attacked, etc., which prepares the way for his receiving either a magical agent or a helper. (THE FIRST FUNCTION OF THE DONOR)
13 The hero reacts to the actions of the future donor. (THE HERO'S REACTION)
14 The hero acquires the use of a magical agent. (PROVISION OR RECEIPT OF A MAGICAL AGENT)
15 The hero is transferred, delivered, or led to the whereabouts of an object of search. (SPATIAL TRANSFERENCE BETWEEN TWO KINGDOMS, GUIDANCE)
16 The hero and the villain join in direct combat. (STRUGGLE)

17 The hero is branded. (BRANDING, MARKING)
18 The villain is defeated. (VICTORY)
19 The initial misfortune or lack is liquidated. (No definition; the peak of narrative, and a pair with 8, VILLAINY)
20 The hero returns. (RETURN)
21 The hero is pursued. (PURSUIT)
22 Rescue of the hero from pursuit. (RESCUE)

A great many tales end here, says Propp, but not all. More complicated fairy-tales have further functions:

23 The hero, unrecognized, arrives home from another country (UNREC-OGNIZED ARRIVAL)
24 A false hero presents unfounded claims. (UNFOUNDED CLAIMS)
25 A difficult task is proposed to the hero. (DIFFICULT TASK)
26 The task is resolved. (SOLUTION)
27 The hero is recognized. (RECOGNITION)
28 The false hero or villain is exposed. (EXPOSURE)
29 The hero is given a new appearance. (TRANSFIGURATION)
30 The villain is punished. (PUNISHMENT)
31 The hero is married and ascends the throne. (WEDDING)

Propp also discerned additional elements of the tale, among which the most interesting is the division of the sphere of action between different characters: the Villain, the Donor, the Helper, a Princess, a Princess's Father, the Dispatcher, the Hero, and the False Hero.

Morphology of evolution theories

Misia Landau (1984; 1991), a paleoanthropologist, observed that the various theories of human evolution can be seen as versions of the universal hero tale in folklore and myth. Having applied Propp's analysis to those texts, she was able to show that the narratives all have a similar, nine-part structure, featuring a humble hero (a non-human primate) who departs on a journey (leaves his natural habitat), receives essential aid or equipment from a donor figure (an evolutionary principle – e.g. natural selection or orthogenesis), goes through tests (imposed by predators, harsh climate, or competitors), and finally arrives at a higher (that is, more human) state. While until this point all evolution theories are ending-embedded – that is, see the emergence of humanity as the purpose of evolution (see the section 'Scripts and schemas') – predicting the future, they hesitate between a happy end or a disaster.

Analyzing both classic and modern tales on evolution, Landau showed not only their common narrative form but also how this form accommodates differences in meaning – that is, widely varying sequences of events, heroes, and donors. Consequently, the interpretations of fossil record differed according to what the paleontologist believed was the donor (that is, the primary evolutionary agent).

Landau's reading confirms Bruner's observation that a narrative is an excellent form for negotiation of meaning. Several of her narrators – Thomas Henry Huxley, Arthur Keith, Elliot Smith – have fought great battles with their opponents (Huxley with Owen, Keith and Smith with one another), never mentioning their names. Instead of engaging in a scientific debate, they tried to 'outnarrate' their competitors.

Her conclusion was that scientists have much to gain from awareness that they are tellers of stories, and that an understanding of narrative can provide tools for creating new scientific theories and analyzing old ones. The aim of her exercise was to liberate paleontology from its conventional narrative corset and open it for new forms of narrative. Indeed, in her next effort (1987), she compared the evolutionary theory to Milton's *Paradise Lost*.

Landau's use of Propp's analysis is instructive because it is extremely conscious of its purpose. As she says herself: '[t]he main purpose in fitting theories of human evolution into a common frame-work is not to demonstrate that they fit' (1991: 11–12). The purposes can be two: either to show that they fit in spite of their diversity, thus upholding traditional cultural values (the case of paleontology); or to show how texts deviate from a generic scheme, thus subverting given cultural values (the case of the nineteenth-century novel, as demonstrated by Jameson, 1981). Just showing that Propp's analysis can be applied to a text does not reveal much.

Actant model

This is why many authors who use structuralist analysis,[3] not the least in the sociology of science and technology, use instead the 'actant model' suggested by the French semiologist of Lithuanian origin, Algirdas Greimas (see, e.g., Greimas and Courtés, 1982). Greimas took Propp's work as a point of departure for developing a model for understanding the organizing principles of all narrative discourses. Somewhat similar to Ricoeur, he distinguished between discursive level (enunciation) and narrative level (utterance), between the ways a narrative is told and a narrative itself.[4]

He introduced the notion of *narrative program*, a change of state produced by any subject affecting any other subject (which is equivalent to the minimal plot, according to Todorov's definition quoted earlier). Narrative programs become chained to one another in a logical succession, thus forming a *narrative trajectory*.

Greimas claims to have revealed a *canonical narrative schema* encompassing three such trajectories:

> the qualification of the subject, which introduces it into life; its 'realization'; by means of which it 'acts'; and finally the sanction – at one and the same time retribution and recognition – which alone guarantees the meaning of its actions and installs it as a subject of being. (Greimas and Courtés, 1982: 204)

Observe the pronoun 'it'; Greimas talks here of a grammatical subject, that might or might not reveal itself as a person. He replaced the term 'character' with the term 'actant' – 'that which accomplishes or undergoes an act' (p. 5), 'since it applies not only to human beings but also to animals, objects, or concepts'. This allows us to notice how actants change role throughout a narrative: an actant might become an actor (acquire a character) or remain an object of somebody else's action. 'Thus the hero will be the hero only in certain parts of the narrative – s/he was not the hero before and s/he may well not be the hero afterwards' (p. 6). 'So defined, the actant is not a concept which is fixed once and for all, but is virtually subsuming an entire narrative trajectory' (p. 207).

These elements of Greimas' version of structuralism made it attractive to the scholars of science and technology, who intended to give more important place to machines and artifacts in their narratives and felt encumbered by the notions of 'actor' and 'action', so clearly assuming a human character and an intentional conduct. 'Actant' and 'narrative program' would do much better; also, as I see it, the universalistic ambitions of Greimas were not of much importance for them.

Accordingly, in the example I quote here, Bruno Latour not so much *applies* Greimas' model as he *uses* it, in the Rortian sense. In this way, he claims, social studies of technology can gain a new narrative resource. In 'Technology is society made durable' (1992), he presents the history of the invention of the Kodak camera and the simultaneous emergence of the mass market for amateur photography as a sequence of programs and anti-programs (from the point of view of Eastman). The following is an example (where capitals denote actants):

> *Program*: professional-amateur (A)/wet collodion (C) **1850**/paper manufacturing (D) *anti-program*: doing everything oneself right away. (Latour, 1992: 111)

While the invention of the wet collodion and the possibilities of paper manufacturing opened new venues of servicing serious amateurs and professional photographers to Eastman, at the same time it has become possible for the photographers to do everything themselves (not exactly in Eastman's interests). Thus Eastman in 1860–70 came up with a new program: producing dry collodion plates made ahead of time, a program that was not counteracted by an anti-program for a good while.

As the narrative proceeds, says Latour, it is marked by two operations: association (called syntagm in narratology) and substitution (paradigm). 'The film is substituted to the plates, and the dry collodion is substituted to the wet collodion, capitalists replace other capitalists, and above all, average consumers replace professional-amateurs' (1992: 113). But the question that interests Latour, and the reason he conducts this Greimasian analysis, is the question of power:

> Is the final consumer forced to buy a Kodak camera? In a sense, yes, since the whole land-scape is now built in such a way that there is no course of action left but to rush to the Eastman company store. However, this domination is visible only at the end of the story. At many other steps in the story the innovation was highly flexible, negotiable, at the mercy of a contingent event. (1992: 113)

This is an important difference between Latour's analysis and a conventional social science's. Latour's reading constructs the story as outcome-embedded: each episode is determined by the outcome of the previous one (see also the next section). Conventional social science is ending-embedded, or teleological (Landau, 1991, quotes paleontology as a typical example).

Thus, concludes Latour, an innovation is but a syntagmatic line (connecting programs to further programs) containing actants – human and non-human – that were recruited to counter the anti-programs. Each time an anti-program emerged or was introduced (e.g. by competitors), Eastman Kodak managed to recruit new actants to their next program. In this way Eastman Kodak has become an important actor – but only at the end of the story. Contrarily to many heroic narratives, there was nothing in the 'character' of Eastman Kodak at the beginning of the story that could help the observer foresee its final success. It was an actant as any other, and it became an actor because it succeeded to recruit many other actants to its cause. But at many time points in the story, Eastman Kodak could have shared the fate of many other entrepreneurs who ended up bankrupt and unknown.

One could therefore summarize the Latourian/Greimasian procedure as fol-lows. It begins with an identification of actants (those who act and are acted upon). Thereupon one follows the actants through a trajectory – a series of programs and anti-programs – until they become actors, that is, acquire a dis-tinct and (relatively) stable character. Which actants have a chance to become actors? Those whose programs succeeded in combating anti-programs (alter-natively, those whose anti-programs won, as in the stories of opposition and resistance). This success, suggests Latour, is due to association: formation and stabilization of networks of actants, who can then present themselves as actor-networks.

Latour uses many more Greimasian concepts in his analysis which is longer and more complex than I present it here. However, I wish to call attention to two aspects of his structuralist analysis. To begin with, Latour does not introduce the whole of Greimas' apparatus – he simply uses bits of it.[5] He does not seem interested in demonstrating his knowledge or skill in using the model: he is using it because the model permits him to say things about his chosen topic – innovation and power – that he would not have been able to say otherwise. At the risk of sounding too normative, I nevertheless want to express a conviction that narrative analysis should be used to elucidate matters of interest in social sciences, and not for the sake of using it. Propp and Greimas have already told us what the canonical structures of narratives are; social scientists must show their consequence in and for social life.

Scripts and schemas

In psychology, the interest in stories, or at least storytelling (enunciation), goes back to Frederick C. Bartlett and his studies of remembering (1932). While Jerome Bruner and Donald E. Polkinghorne brought narrative back into psychology in its literary version, cognitive psychologists were developing the notion of scripts (see, e.g., Schank and Abelson, 1977) and schema (Mandler, 1984).

Jean Matter Mandler suggests that it is important to distinguish a story grammar and a story schema:

> A story grammar is a rule system devised for the purpose of describing the regulari-
> ties found in one kind of text. The rules describe the units of which stories are com-
> posed, that is, their constituent structure, and the ordering of the units, that is, the
> sequences in which the constituents appear. A story schema, on the other hand, is a
> mental structure consisting of sets of expectations about the way in which stories pro-
> ceed. (1984: 18)

In my reading, a story grammar is the analysis of the text, a search for *intentio operis*, or a semiotic strategy; a story schema is the repertoire of plots typical for a certain interpretive community.

Mandler gives an example of the analysis of story grammar where she uses categories inspired by Propp, extended and reformulated (1984: 22–30). Like other structuralists, Mandler assumes that all stories have a basic structure that remains relatively unchanged in spite of the differences in the content of various stories:

1   A setting, which introduces a protagonist and other characters, and statements about the time and place of the story. One or more episodes that form a plot of the story. They also have a similar structure:

2   Episode(s):

2A a beginning (one or more events)

2B a development:

- – the reaction of a protagonist: simple (anger, fear) or complex. If complex, it is followed by
- – the setting of a goal (what to do about the beginning event(s)),
- – a goal path, an outcome (success or failure)

2C The ending, including a commentary: concerning the consequences of the episode, or the protagonist's or the narrator's reflection. The ending of the final episode becomes

3 The ending, which might also contain a moral lesson.

Episodes can be temporally or causally connected (the two rules of association). There are two kinds of causal connections. The first is ending-embedded: the end reveals the substitution, or the transformation – for example, a new protagonist–goal combination (after the suitor saved the heroine's life she understands she always loved him). The second is outcome-embedded: the structure of the story and the connections between episodes depend on the episode's outcome and therefore they can change during the narrative (for example, a hero who failed starts a different chain of episodes or an anti-program). In Hayden White's terms, these are the standard ways of emplotment. As suggested in the previous sections, ending-embedded plots are typical of conventional social science theories, whereas outcome-embedded plots typify theories that allow for contingencies.

Mandler and her collaborators then proceeded to a series of experiments aimed at testing both cognitive structures and recall. In one of the experiments they built three types of stories (temporal, ending-embedded, and outcome-embedded) but presented the elements as unconnected (omitting 'and', 'then', and even punctuation marks). The subjects connected the stories, sometimes following the standard grammar (a 'canonical' version), and sometimes providing alternative structures (i.e. schema). In another experiment, one version of the story presented it in a schematic version (in this case, temporal), while the other presented the story in a way that interleaved its episodes ('…meanwhile'). In recall of the interleaved story, many subjects (and especially children) reconstructed a schematic story rather than the story they actually heard (both stories were perfectly understandable). (Please bear this experiment in mind when reading the next chapter.)

Other kinds of structural analysis

Although structuralist analyses are best known they are not the only kind of structural analysis of narratives. Such analyses are made in many disciplines, from literary theory to linguistics to semiotics to ethnomethodology. In fact, as pointed out Latour (1993a), semiotics can be seen as an ethnomethodology of texts, an analogy that is easy to accept if one assumes, after Ricoeur, that a text is a written fragment of a discourse.

Narrative analysis also constitutes part of rhetorical analysis: *narratio* is the second part of a six-part classical oration (see also Chapter 9). Kenneth Burke's *pentad* (Scene, Actor, Agency, Act, and Purpose) that stems from the rhetorical tradition has been much used in social sciences (Burke, 1968; Overington, 1977a; 1997b; Mangham and Overington, 1987; Czarniawska, 1997) and I shall return to it in Chapter 8. In my own narrative analysis, I am especially attracted to the work of Tzvetan Todorov, very likely because his way of writing appeals to me most (I do believe that an affinity with an author facilitates the use of his or her method). Todorov is a literary theorist and thus a specialist in a subject that I am more familiar with than semiotics or linguistics, and he uses a structuralist analysis in a non-formalized way, borrowing freely from Propp and Greimas but not following either of them exactly.

In a Foreword to Todorov's *The Poetics of Prose* the US literary theoretician Jonathan Culler summarized it very succinctly: 'When poetics studies individual works, it seeks not to interpret them but to discover the *structures and conventions* of literary discourse, *which enable them to have the meanings they do*' (Culler, 1977: 8, emphasis added). Change the adjective 'literary' to 'social' and this is a program that seems to me perfectly feasible in social sciences.

Todorov is especially interested in plot structure. This is still in agreement with Propp and Greimas in the sense that actors – or characters – are results of actions, and not of single actions either but of a series of actions. Actants become 'characters' if they manage to keep the same (or the same but transformed) role through a series of actions; or, in Greimasian terms, if their performance leads to acquisition of a competence. But a series of actions remains such only in an incomplete narrative or in a narrative composed by temporal or spatial vicinity; in a story or a complete narrative, the connections are the result of the work of emplotment. Therefore it is the plot that is a central feature of a narrative and it is a plot that will produce the characters. A clown seen in an opening scene will turn into a tragic character if the play is a tragedy (possibly, tragicomic). What deserves attention, therefore, is the kind of connections between episodes.

Here I quote a story that one of my interlocutors in Stockholm told me about the water and sewers management in the city (Czarniawska, 2002). Like many stories, it starts with a description of a state of affairs so bad that it had to be changed:

(Dis)equilibrium 1

In the 19th century Stockholm was besieged with sickness, with epidemics. People had all kinds of stomach diseases and the cause was clear: the primitive handling of water, and drinking of dirty water. Thus the city witnessed epidemics of cholera and many other diseases that today are to be found only in developing countries, high infant mortality etc.

Action 1
The solution was to build waterworks, which was accomplished by the turn of the century. The next step was the sewers,

Equilibrium 1
and this was a revolution, a revolution in hygiene. It was fantastic, the way one solved society's hygiene problems.

Complication 1
But later on it became clear that the problems were pushed away, and not really solved. Water in lakes and the sea had become so polluted that it was impossible to bathe there anymore.

Action 2
It was then that the first purification plants started to be built.
The first purification plant, using mechanical devices, was opened in Stockholm in 1934. In 1941 a second, bigger one was built; the third in 1950.

Equilibrium 2
After that, purification techniques became better and better. Later on, water treatment has been built up and improved. In the 1960s the focus fell on environmental issues. The first environment protection law was enforced in Sweden in 1969. It was extremely helpful for improving the situation of discharges and consequently diminishing the pollution of nature in general and water in particular.

Complication 2
But society was becoming more and more complex. You can see yourself how the traffic increases all the time, and how elements dangerous to the environment – biocides and fungicides – create more and more problems.

Action 3
All this has found its expression during the famous Rio conference that adopted the concept of 'sustainable development', coined by the Brundtland committee. All participating heads of state signed the Rio declaration, so that the attention paid to the issues of environment became quite different.

Equilibrium 3
Today we talk not about environmental protection, but in terms of sustainability, in terms of circulation and natural resource management. This is a much wider perspective that sets much higher demands. The level of difficulty has increased seriously.

Stockholm Water is a typical example of an environmental engineering company. It is precisely in this type of company that the notion of a long horizon, of sustainable development, is most central ... There is a holistic view of things. We see water in Stockholm as a natural resource that is on loan to us. We take it to fulfill the city's needs, but then we must see to it that the water is purified in such a way that it can be given back, can enter the natural circulation without any damage. And this is what we work with: to improve, to optimize this system. (Stockholm, Observation 5/1)

This seems to be a pretty standard story: whenever the equilibrium is upset, an action is taken to restore it; when complications ensue, they, too, are taken care of. But there are certain original features of this story.

To begin with, it is not easy to make a complete list of actants: the 'water people', local and global, are obvious enough; so is 'the city' and the 'polluters' (human and non-human), but who, or what, stands behind the complications, or anti-programs? Who, possibly apart from city authorities, stands for programs? There seem to exist three actants, grammatically practically absent (with one exception, Complication 2: '*society* was becoming more and more complex'): Society, Nature, and Science. Both Society and Nature stand, albeit unintentionally, for anti-programs: Science stands for all positive programs, although that is not mentioned.

I would like to claim that this is a kind of narrative that Propp could not have found in the collection of fairytales because it is a *modern story*. It has two standard actants, which could change their character even within the same story: society and nature can bring about problems or solutions. The third important actant, Science, ends invariably in a modern story in the way partly similar to Fate in ancient stories, as it cannot be resisted. It differs from Fate in its trajectory, though. Science comes to no end and achieves no equilibrium; it continues forward and upward in a constant progress. The plot in a modern story relies on these two devices: society and nature cause disequilibria, and science restores equilibrium, on a for ever higher level. This is yet another evolution story in an upbeat version.

EXERCISE

Exercise 6.1: structural analysis

Attempt a structural analysis of 'My life so far'.

FURTHER READING

Cooren, François (2000) *The Organizing Property of Communication.* Amsterdam: John Benjamins.
Mandler, Jean Matter (1984) *Stories, Scripts, and Scenes: Aspects of Schema Theory.* Hillsdale, NJ: Lawrence Erlbaum Associates.
Mishler, Elliot G. (1986) *Research Interviewing. Context and Narrative.* Cambridge, MA: Harvard University Press.
Propp, Vladimir (1928/1968) *Morphology of the Folktale.* Austin, TX: University of Texas Press.

Notes

1 Propp makes a series of affirmations concerning 'all fairytales' which are highly problematic but not especially relevant in the present context.

2 Here is an example (I took the one that was easiest on my keyboard):

Analysis of a simple, single move tale of class H-I, of the type: kidnapping of a person.

131. A tsar, three daughters. (α). The daughters go walking (β^3), overstay in the garden (δ^1). A dragon kidnaps them (A^1). A call for aid (B^1). Quest of three heroes ($C\uparrow$). Three battles with the dragon (H^1-I^1), rescue of the maidens (K^4). Return ($\downarrow$), reward ($W°$).

$$\beta^3\delta^1A^1B^1C\uparrow H^1\text{-}I^1K^4\downarrow W°$$

(Propp, 1968: 128)

3 For example, Donna Haraway (1992), Catherine Hayles (1993), François Cooren (2000; 2001), Daniel Robichaud (2003), and Anne-Marie Søderberg (2003). See also Timothy Lenoir (1994) for a cautionary voice.

4 I do not think it is incorrect to see reading as a kind of enunciation, although it might bring different theories too close to one another for their authors.

5 He does not even quote Greimas – it is known from his other texts that he uses him as an inspiration (see, e.g., Latour, 1988; 1993a). Such a move is not recommended to young scholars but it further indicates that a use of a specific model is not the point.

7

Close Readings: Poststructuralism, Interruption, Deconstruction

Almost before structuralism acquired legitimacy in the social sciences, it was swept away by poststructuralism. The move from structuralism to poststructuralism was not as dramatic as it may seem. It meant, above all, abandoning 'the depth' for 'the surface': if deep structures are demonstrable, they must be observable. Structures could no longer be 'found', as they were obviously put into the text – by those who read the text, including the author (after all, reading is writing anew). This meant abandoning the idea of the universal structure of language, or of mind, and accepting the idea of a common repertoire of textual strategies, which are recognizable to both the writer and the reader. Such relaxation of basic assumptions also led to the relaxation of the technique: as there is no one true deep structure to be discovered, various techniques can be applied to structure a text and therefore permit its novel reading.

Instead of pursuing a dogmatic treatment of deconstruction, in this chapter it is treated on a par with other ways of 'interrogating' a text: the chapter contains a review of approaches that, albeit launched under different names, have in common the same intention of finding out 'what a text does' rather than 'what it says', to borrow Silverman and Torode's distinction (1980).

Poststructuralism in action

The example of the use of poststructuralism I want to quote here is both unusual and highly instructive. An Australian sociologist, Bronwyn Davies, was interested in how people learn their gender: her starting point was the assumption that children learn to become male or female and that they do so through learning discursive practices in which all people are positioned as either male or female (Davies, 1989).[1] She adopted poststructuralism as her own discourse (in the sense of vocabulary) because it provided her with the conceptual tools − devices − to make sense of her material, allowing her to formulate answers to the questions that started her inquiry. She chose it because it is a radical discourse which 'allows us to think beyond the male–female dualism as inevitable, to the constitutive processes through which we position ourselves as male or female and which we can change if we so choose' (1989: xi).

This is to me an excellent rationale behind a choice of an approach. At any given time there are several approaches, or vocabularies, that are in principle equally applicable to a given inquiry. What Foucauldians call 'discourse', the new institutionalists call 'meaning system'. The choice is actually an active matching process. It is easier to apply a narrative approach to a material composed of texts written with words, but it can also be applied to texts written with numbers. There are quite a few authors propagating the structuralist approach, as I showed in the previous chapter, but some social scientists opt for a linguistic variation of structuralism, some for a semiotic one, some, like myself, for the literary, and still others decide to make their own mixture. Fashion, authority, aesthetic responses all play a role in the choice of an approach, and so do logical arguments. As Davies points out, she needed a radical approach, as she set out to problematize one of the things most taken for granted.

One part of Davies' inquiry (I will not be able to report here the whole of it) concerned reading a variety of feminist revisions of well-known fairytales to seven four- and five-year-old children. She spent many hours with each child during a period of one year, reading the stories and discussing what they thought of each of the stories. One of the stories was a variation of the well-known 'princess rescued from the dragon by the prince' story. It went as follows:

> At the beginning of the story, Princess Elizabeth and Prince Ronald are planning to get married, but then the dragon comes along, burns Elizabeth's castle and clothes and flies off into the distance carrying Prince Ronald by the seat of his pants. Elizabeth is very angry. She finds a paper bag to wear and follows the dragon. She tricks him into displaying all of his magic powers until he falls asleep from exhaustion. She rushes into the dragon's cave to save Ronald only to find that he does not want to be saved by a princess who is covered in soot and only has an old paper bag to wear. Elizabeth is quite taken aback by this turn of events, and she says: 'Ronald, your clothes are really pretty and your hair is very neat. You look like a real prince, but you are a bum.' The last pages show her skipping off into the sunset alone and the story ends with the words: 'They didn't get married after all.' (1989: viii)

In the discussions afterwards, the three girls placed themselves in the position of the princess, whom they saw as nice and beautiful. They all understood Elizabeth's plan and concluded that Ronald was not nice. One of them, however, believed that Elizabeth should have done as Ronald told her (he tells her to go away, get changed, and come back when she looks more like a real princess).

Among the four boys, three of them wanted to be in the position of the prince. Two of them believed the prince was clever; the third boy did not think the prince was nice but still wanted to be like him. The fourth boy recognized the prince as 'not very good' and 'stupid' and wanted to be the dragon, 'the smartest and fiercest dragon in the whole world'. Although the boys understood Elizabeth's plan, they all refused her the position as the central character, attributing it to Ronald or the dragon. The two boys who saw Ronald as clever argued, for example, that 'Ronand very cleverly holds on to his tennis racquet tightly which is why he stays up in the air' (p. 61) and that 'He's got a tennis jumper and he won the tennis gold medal' (p. 62). All the boys are concerned with Elizabeth's looks: she is 'messy', 'messy and dirty', 'yucky'. 'I'd tell her "You look dumb with your old paper bag on"' (p. 62). There were many clues, says Davies, that it was not dirt but Elizabeth's temporary nakedness that was the central problem, although it remained unspoken. Whichever way, this is an exemplification of the intricate connection between mimesis and a plot, mentioned in Chapter 2: the description of the princess as dirty permitted and justified a certain type of plot.

Davies regrouped the children not according to gender but according to whether they understood that Elizabeth is the hero of the story and that Ronald is not nice. It turned out that the four children who understood the feminist interpretation of the story had employed mothers, and their fathers assumed a greater than average share of domestic duties. The three children who saw Elizabeth's action as aiming at getting her prince back and saving her future marriage had mothers who were housewives, although two of them were well educated.

Davies points out that it would be a mistake to see a connection between children's ability to imagine women as active agents in the public world and mothers' employment as causal. If there were such a connection, the solution to gender inequality would simply be sending all women to work. 'But going out to work is not necessarily accompanied by discursive practices in which the work the woman undertakes is seen as giving her agency or power' (p. 64). Indeed, being able to compare an all-female and all-male team working in basically the same position in city administration in Warsaw and Stockholm, I was struck by the difference in the ways they talked during their job and about their job. While men were obviously convinced of both the difficulty and importance of their work, women talked in the same way (and often interminglingly) about their tasks and about their last summer holidays or knitting.

In the second year of her study, Davies kept visiting a number of preschool and childcare centers in order to observe the way children talked and acted in their everyday lives. Reading stories was part of it and, although the discussions were not very extensive, they brought about more interpretations of *The Paperbag Princes*, some of them with an openly sexual context. Nevertheless, the dominating line in interpretations was that of a romantic love. For boys, Elizabeth is in error when presenting herself to the prince dirty and naked. They expect her actions to be demonstrating her goodness and virtue, but they see it as Ronald's right to refuse it as insufficient. The girls are baffled by Elizabeth's refusal of Ronald whom she loved at the outset, and at her decision to control her own life. After all, there is no room in a traditional romantic plot for selfish thoughts and anger: 'The power of the pre-existing structure of the traditional narrative to prevent a new form of narrative from being heard is ever-present', concludes Davies (1989: 69). And, as Jean Matter Mandler could have told her, the traditional narratives are easier to recall.

Interruption

David Silverman and Brian Torode (1980) earlier pointed out that developments in linguistics, semiotics, and literary theory could be of more general significance for social scientists than just for specific fields like socio-linguistics. They pointed out the closeness between ethnomethodology and semiotics before Latour did, and they were against differentiating between discourse and narrative, enunciation and utterance, conversation and text: all these could be approached similarly. Without referring to him, they were in agreement with de Certeau (1984/1988) that there is no clear separation line between writing and reading, or between text production and text consumption. They choose, instead, to oppose interpretation to interruption (in terms used in Chapter 5, explication to explanation) or the question 'what does a text say?' to the question 'how does a text say it?':

> The language of interruption approaches another text or conversation with the aim of interrogating the relation between appearance and reality that is proposed there. It seeks to discover and support the anti-authoritarian practices within ordinary language which interpretation opposes and represses. By rejecting any appeal to idealist 'essences' outside ordinary language, interruption represents a materialist turn towards the character of linguistic practices themselves. (Silverman and Torode, 1980: xi–xii)

In a more benevolent reading of interpretation-as-explication, suggested throughout this book, it is possible both to interpret and interrogate the same text. I have therefore applied what I called 'an interruptive interpretation' to the stories I collected in the power study mentioned in Chapter 2 (Czarniawska-Joerges, 1994). True, I reduced the texts simply by translating them into English. This amounts to treating a text as an appearance, changing which will not affect the reality behind it. But I did not look for the 'reality behind': instead, I observed that the texts themselves used the appearance–reality contrast as their own devices. The 'how' was at the service of the 'what': people are skillful narrative makers. Consequently, I was able to show what the texts did by a specific way of saying of what they were saying: the 'second-order what' through the 'how of the what', so to speak. I here quote some of the stories and give them titles that already announce the conclusion of my 'interruptive interpretation':[2]

Anti-feminist discourse: a Polish student
A weeping woman was sitting in front of the desk, nervously uncrossing and recrossing her legs. Behind the desk, which was entirely covered with paper, sat an official talking in a high voice. It appeared that the woman had an overdue bill for electricity and water which she promised to pay. However, she couldn't pay it immediately because of temporary financial problems. She promised to pay the bill in installments or next month. I thought the solution seemed acceptable, but the official reacted sharply and remarked sarcastically that his [*? in original gender unclear, BC*] role was collecting dues, not looking for new solutions to people's private problems.

In this story, we meet the narrator (a woman) and two protagonists: a woman who is a victim of bureaucratic power and an oppressor whose biological gender is hidden from the reader. In fact, it was the text that interrupted my reading, not the other way around. Attempting to translate a text written in Polish into English, I realized that, while a stylistic requirement calls for the use of a personal pronoun rather than a repetition of the noun, I did not know which pronoun to use. I met this difficulty in Polish stories over and over again: sometimes even the biological gender of the victim was hidden and could be guessed only when the victim was the narrator (who indicated her sex in response to a formal request included in the instruction).

My 'interruptive interpretation' led me to a hypothesis (a guess in another vocabulary) that the students hid the gender of the protagonists because they wanted their stories to be about power, not about gender relations. In the story above, if the oppressor was a woman, the story could be read as an example of 'women being nasty to one another' (the hidden assumption being that men do not do this to each other) – a popular story in organizations, as I discovered. If the oppressor were a man, this would become a 'feminist story', which is self-condemning. In an amazing work, *The World without Women: Gender in Public Life in Poland*, Agnieszka Graff (2001) shows a collective agreement visible in Poland (and in other East European countries) that the 'women's issue' is not only unimportant but also possibly threatening to the enterprise of building a liberal democracy. This attitude, like the story itself, reaches back earlier than 1989. Under the socialist regime, the women's issue was seen as threatening to the solidarity of the opposition movement and feminism as belonging to the discourse of the oppressor.

A-feminist discourse: a Finnish story

My working day ended at 16.15. Managing Director was on holiday. At 16.20, exactly when I was ready to go home, he came in and demanded that I type for him a table seat order. I would gladly point out to him the time, explain that I am in a hurry, and also emphasize that he was asking me to do something for his private use. But I knew his power, felt his authoritative glance and began to type.

He waited, mentioned how long a time it was taking and banged his fingers on the table. When I was ready he took the sheet, looked at it and said, coldly: 'No, this is not how I want it. You must retype it.'

I did. Three times. It was 17.30 when I left. I behaved as my secretary's role required because I did not dare to oppose his incredible way of exploiting his position of power.

The gender of the protagonists is clear (the male superior, the female secretary) but not made much of: they simply represent two categories, the powerful and the powerless. This is how things go in organizations. Another, similar, story ended with the following comment: 'But normally, one does not reflect much upon such situations. If one wants to work for people who have power, it is best to let them exercise their power. Otherwise, as a secretary, one will not stay long.'

A similar picture was found in many stories. It has been commented on in two different ways: 'This is how it is – and it is best to get used to it' versus 'This is how it must not be – and it is a shame that it is so.' What 'it' is that people in organizations are often helpless, and this is usually related to age (sometimes biological, sometimes organizational) and gender. The most obvious frame of reference for these stories would be that of the patriarchate: what else do age and gender together amount to? But such a feminist interpretation was nowhere to be seen in the accounts. One possible explanation could be found in such texts as Simonen (1991: 51–2): 'Finnish women were of great importance in political and economic life both during and – unlike their sisters in many other Western countries – also after the war ... Since the Second World War, the education of girls has been more common than that of boys in the Finnish countryside.'

The official picture is therefore of exceptionally advanced equality (the first country in Europe to give women the franchise, 1909) – indeed, a privileged position for women. Only recently is there a growing host of interpretations that point out that the present 'power distribution' was built up during the war at the front (Eräsaari, 2002). Even if Finnish women ran factories, public offices, and families during the war, the 'old boys' came back from the front with a ready network and simply took over, fostering a new generation of 'crown princes'. In the stories told in the study, the tension between the official version of reality and the experiential one is solved by depicting the events in terms of patriarchal situations, but not analyzing them in those terms. A very different textual strategy has been found in Italian accounts:

Feminist discourse: an Italian narrative

The new head of the office lacked experience of the area in question, having come from a professional background of a very different type than what was required for running this particular office. He decided to organize and to manage both the personnel and the office as an entirely bureaucratic structure, filled with rituals. The personnel found themselves forced to operate in a style which differed significantly from the previous setup. The consequences were mobilization on the one hand, and lack of communication on the other.

The style of the new boss, which was directed toward seducing as many of his collaborators as possible, brought results after a few months. The clothes of some people became more ceremonial, more formal. Those of the women – more seductive. And so the battle between professionality and sexuality had begun.

The new boss, a man of good looks, did not hide his openly chauvinist attitude, calling women 'Mrs.' and 'Miss',... quite different from 'Doctor' or 'Professor'.

Thus, bureaucracy and ceremony toward the male professionals, and what about women? Those who felt marginalized by the previous management for being too talented, and therefore too dangerous, thought they had finally found a space for themselves. Soon, however, this space began to shrink. Alliances, double alliances and intrigues invaded the camp ...

This event, where I was involved up to a point, illustrates how, even in today's organizations, the role of a professional woman is far from unproblematic. This is especially visible when power, with its various mechanisms, tries to increase the boundaries between the male and the female, as if they were two separate territories, to be conquered, one by professionality (if only superficial) and another by sheer sexuality.

As you can see, I used the word 'narrative' and not 'story' in the title of the excerpt: indeed, although the narrator speaks of 'an event', there is hardly one. The text is already an interpretation, and an interruptive one at that. The narrator places herself 'within the gap of "rupture" between formulations of "appearance" and "reality"' (Silverman and Torode, 1980: 1960). She is a postgraduate student of sociology and analyzes her work experience in the language of feminism, which happens to be a legitimate discourse in her group, and she speaks from a woman's standpoint (Smith, 1987). But this is hardly a legitimate discourse or a typical standpoint in mainstream organizational

TABLE 7.1   *What do the texts say and what do the texts do?*

	Polish	Finnish	Italian
What the texts say			
Appearance	Bureaucratic rules	Organizational order	Bureaucratic and organizational order
Reality	Oppression	Exploitation	Sexism and manipulation
What the texts do	Expose hypocrisy (call in a moral dimension)	Establish normalcy and exception	Expose instrumentality of seduction (call in a political dimension)

Source: Czarniawska-Joerges (1994: 244).

sociology. Until recently, the issues of sexuality were a taboo in discourse on organizations, taken up only in 'subversive discourses' or explicitly in critical stances, such as Burrell (1984) or Gherardi (1995).

The Italian students (male and female) openly declared their fundamentally critical and political stance when judging organizational practices. It was interesting to compare their accounts to those of the Finnish students who raised the issue of gender in spite of their relatively apologetic way of describing organizations. Additionally, gender in the Finnish accounts was seen as an individual and biological attribute (certain employees are female and certain employees are young) that acquired a social meaning only in a specific context. Furthermore, gender was not related to sexuality. (I have summarized my interruptive interpretation in Table 7.1.)

I found this exercise in interruption interesting and fruitful. I have learned from it two further lessons concerning narrative analysis. To begin with, social scientists (and semioticians, literary critics, linguists) are not the only ones who interpret, interrogate, and interrupt texts. All people do it, some more often some less often; the world is full of semiotic readers. Reading a semiotic reading is an interesting challenge, somewhat dizzying and requiring a lot of caution, but nevertheless very satisfying. The caution concerns the necessity of a symmetrical stance, as it were: the awareness that the authors of the text that social scientists analyze may turn out even more skillful analysts themselves. The dizziness comes from an attempt to keep a balance between standing under, over, and for – the analyzed text. The 'natural attitude' of a social scientist is to stand over, to explain (as I did above), but an admiring explication is an attitude to be applied more often.

The second lesson concerns the matter of language. Although practically all narratologists set the constitutive role of language in the central place, the issue of analyzing narratives in a foreign language does not attract much attention. Even such reflective authors as Silverman and Torode assume that translation is unproblematic. But it certainly is highly problematic – especially in this kind of analysis. One solution to this difficulty is to make a literal translation first and an understandable translation afterwards. It makes for a lot of annotations, often making the text incomprehensible. Another solution is to translate only the result of the analysis (as I was doing), hoping for the reader's suspension of disbelief, in spite of a referential contract with the reader. But the fact that it is difficult should not be read as the reason not to undertake this kind of translation – it must be remembered that the origins of semiotics go back to comparative linguistics and that comparative linguistics was a product of necessity. Jan Baudouin de Courtney, one of its founders (Jakobson, 1978), was a Pole of French origins who lived and worked in Estonia and Russia, teaching in Russian and German.

Deconstruction

> To 'deconstruct' a text is to draw out conflicting logics of sense and implication, with the object of showing that the text never exactly means what it says or says what it means. (Norris, 1988: 7)

Deconstruction is a technique and a philosophy of reading, characterized by a preoccupation with desire and power. Used by Jacques Derrida (1976; 1987) for reading philosophical texts, it becomes a kind of philosophy itself (Rorty, 1989). Used by gender scholars, it becomes a tool of subversion (Johnson, 1980). Used by organization researchers, it becomes a technique of reading by estrangement (Feldman, 1995). As a technique of reading, it earns an excellent introduction in Joanne Martin's article 'Deconstructing organizational taboos' (1990).

Martin attended a conference sponsored by a major US university dedicated to the ways that individuals and businesses might help to solve societal problems. One of the participants, the CEO of a large transnational organization, told the conference participants the following story:

> We have a young woman who is extraordinarily important to the launching of a major new [product]. We will be talking about it next Tuesday in its first worldwide introduction. She has arranged to have her Caesarian yesterday in order to be prepared for this event, so you – We have insisted that she stay home and this is going to be televised in a closed circuit television, so we're having this done by TV for her, and she is staying home three months and we are finding ways of filling in to create this void for us because we think it's an important thing for her to do. (Martin, 1990: 339)

Unlike stories exemplified in Chapter 2, this one was found disembedded from its original context and recontextualized into the space of the conference. Accordingly, instead of following its connections through time and space, Martin has decided to deconstruct and reconstruct the story from a feminist standpoint (the alternative standpoints were, for example, the political leftist or the rationalist). She composed a list of deconstructionist moves. This list, apart from being a useful aid to anyone who would like to try a hand at deconstruction, also reveals the historical roots of deconstruction or, rather, its historical sediments. It contains elements of close reading, of rhetorical analysis, of dramatist analysis, of radical rewriting – it is a hybrid. Therefore, it does not make much sense to speak about 'proper deconstruction' or the 'correct use of structural analysis': the literary techniques should serve as a source of inspiration not a prescription to be followed literally.

Analytic strategies used in deconstruction [(Adapted from Martin, 1990: 355)]

1 Dismantling a dichotomy, exposing it as a false distinction (e.g. public/private, nature/culture, etc.).
2 Examining silences – what is not said (e.g. noting who or what is excluded by the use of pronouns such as 'we').
3 Attending to disruptions and contradictions; places where a text fails to make sense or does not continue.
4 Focusing on the element that is most alien or peculiar in the text – to find the limits of what is conceivable or permissible.
5 Interpreting metaphors as a rich source of multiple meanings.
6 Analyzing double entendres that may point to an unconscious subtext, often sexual in content.
7 Separating group-specific and more general sources of bias by 'reconstructing' the text with substitution of its main elements.

Let me give short examples of Martin's deconstruction:

1 Public/private dichotomy: 'We have a young woman…' (rather than: a young woman works for us). The text itself shows the company's awareness that this division cannot be maintained, revealing at the same time that 'woman is to private as man is to public', and that actions intended as improvement in the private sphere turn out to be serving the public sphere; in other words, the public sphere invades the private under the aegis of 'helping'.
2 Silenced voices: 'We insisted that she stayed home…' One voice that is never heard is the physician's voice, although it could be expected in this context. The woman is given a voice ('She arranged to have her Caesarean yesterday…') but it is unclear whether she did it on suggestion from the company or spontaneously. The final word is the company's: '*We* insisted.'
3 Disruptions: '… we are finding ways of filling in to create this void for us.' This incoherence, points out Martin, happens at the point where the costs of the arrangement are taken up in the text, thus revealing the speaker's ambivalence as to the benefits of the situation.
4 The element most alien: pregnancy, says Martin, is an alien element in a male-dominated organization. The visibility of pregnancy calls attention to a whole series of organizational taboos: emotional expression and nurturance, sexual intercourse.

5 Metaphors: child as a product, product as a child ('Why a product can be launched and a baby cannot'; p. 351).
6 Double entendres: 'We have a young woman...'
7 Reconstruction: Martin creates several, and I am quoting only one that I found most poignant, achieved by changing the gender of the protagonist and, consequently, a type of operation:

> We have a young man who is extraordinarily important to the launching of a major new [product]. We will be talking about it next Tuesday in its first worldwide introduction. He has arranged to have his coronary bypass operation yesterday in order to be prepared for this event, so you – We have insisted that he stay home and this is going to be televised in a closed circuit television, so we're having this done by TV for him, and he is staying home three months and we are finding ways of filling in to create this void for us because we think it's an important thing for him to do.

The absurdity of this reconstructed text corroborates what the deconstruction revealed: evidence of a suppressed gender conflict in work organizations, blind spots of management practice, and theory that fueled the conflict and kept it out of view.

Changing worlds

I end with an example of deconstruction of a short excerpt from a Swedish business weekly from 1994. The text has been provided, together with its deconstruction, by Pia Höök from Stockholm School of Economics, and I thank her for permission to use it. I have extended and developed Pia's original deconstruction.[3]

Sordid gain rather than long-term planning

The managers of the small company TrustPhone [*the name has been changed*], which sells security systems for credit cards to the tune of $ 250 ml per year, are truly the 'electronic highway robbers'. They plug in their portables wherever they can find a telephone jack available, or even do it in secret when they cannot get access – after all, the cellular phones are still too expensive for such purposes. There is no head office – there is only the central computer which must be contacted as often as possible. It is via the 'head computer' that everybody cooperates and communicates. Management meetings in person take place every second month or so. The costs are almost nonexistent and profits are accordingly high.

... The message to the employees is: Forget job security! The only thing one can do is to hold oneself 'employable' to many different companies or else pay in fat insurance premiums against unemployment. Specialized knowledge opens the door to high pay, but as often as not, it is a matter of learning more, taking more responsibility, working harder and earning less. The good side of it all is that many people, irrespective of their skin color, nationality, or social background, can break through and have a job where they have more control and responsibility than ever before. Knowledge workers have power in this company. The bad side is that many cannot handle these demands. They join the others in a fight over who will serve hamburgers, clean houses, or take care of children – all with a very low pay.

1 Sordid gain/long-term planning: the very title reveals the journalist's ambivalence about the events described in the text. Sordid gain–long-term investment is a time-honored dichotomy, where the first part is negative and the second positive. The article intends to question this moral dichotomy, proposing the possibility of a reversal.

2 Silenced voices: employees. The whole text is presented from the point of view of managers, with the narrator's voice audible in textual strategies, the choice of metaphors, etc. The employees' point of view is guessed – either by managers or by the journalist.

3 Disruptions: 'Knowledge workers have power in this company. The bad side is that many cannot handle these demands.' The last sentence should have followed a much earlier one ('it is a matter of learning more…') but, in its present context, it seems that knowledge workers cannot handle the demands created by having power. This additionally reveals the journalist's ambivalence, which might be caused by reflection over his own work situation – are knowledge workers interested in having power?

4 The element most alien: plugging in your portable in secret is certainly a novelty in official commercial practice. But the next sentence justifies it with 'After all, the cellular phones are still too expensive for such purposes'. This exotic behavior and its justification are explained by the main metaphor of the text:

5 Metaphors: 'electronic highway robbers.' This is a very congruent metaphor as the heroes of the text are, in fact, stealing. But the interesting aspect of, and yet another proof of, the journalist's ambivalence is that 'highway robbers' are traditionally positive heroes who take from the rich to give to the poor. Who are the rich and who are the poor? Perhaps credit card owners, 'the average citizens', are the poor. Who are the rich? The most likely place to find a telephone jack is some kind of a public space – do they therefore steal from the taxpayer to give it to the customer? Or do they steal for their own benefit?

6 Double entendres: (cannot be analyzed as this is a translation).

7 Reconstruction: the following reconstruction simply reverses the message, leading to the following text:

Long-term planning rather than sordid gain
The managers of the small company TrustComputer, which sells user-friendly computer courses and has 40 employees, are, like everybody else in the company, partners in profits as well as in work. They put their

portables at the client's service wherever they are needed, or even organize courses at their own company if the client cannot afford it – after all, advanced computer equipment is still too expensive for many to purchase. Indeed, theirs is an open office where clients can arrive at any time with their problems. Personal communication and close cooperation are their maxims – inside and outside the company. Management meetings are informal but very frequent – they like each other and appreciate highly the frequent exchange of experiences. No wonder that the personnel turnover is almost nonexistent and competence is high and constantly developing.

... The message to the employees is: we shall not forget how important job security is! The only thing one has to do is to keep oneself up-to-date with the rapid developments on the computer market, which in itself is a fat insurance premium against bad times. Specialized knowledge opens the door to high pay but, as often as not, it is a matter of being able to learn and to unlearn. It is being said that knowledge gives power. In this sense, TrustComputer is the best example of a successful empowerment program, as many people, irrespective of their skin color, nationality, or social background, can acquire power simply by following their life's passion. As the company guarantees their employment, they can spend all their time on acquiring knowledge in order to serve their clients, with the same feeling of usefulness as experienced by those who serve food or take care of children.

What seemed to be an innocent play with a text ended up as a confrontation of the message typical for the welfare state and workplace democracy with the message typical for the (then) coming new economy. A short newspaper text, intended to report somewhat exotic work practices, revealed (not least through the journalist's ambivalence) that at stake were two different world and work philosophies. The new one was to challenge the old one, with the result uncertain, even to the narrator.

At the end of this chapter it is important to point out that both structural and poststructural analyses meant an important turn of the traditional hermeneutics: they managed to change the central question from 'what does a text say?' to 'how does a text say it?' Scholars skeptical toward narrative analyses are still not convinced, though, since to them one more question remains: why? Why do people tell stories? Why do they tell this type of story at this time and at this place? Why do they tell stories this way?

These are questions the answer to which lies in a theory of a phenomenon, not in an analysis of a text. The kind of answer depends, in the first place, on the aim of the study: is it to understand the nature of humankind? The reaction to the collapse of a new economy? The way people make sense of their lives? In the second place, it will depend on the theoretical affiliation of the scholar: the objectivists will refer the answer to relations of power, the subjectivists to the workings of the human mind, and the constructivists will show that the 'how' contains a 'why'. In other words, a narrative analysis forms another narrative that, in order to become a fully fledged story, needs to be emplotted. Theory is the plot of a dissertation. Therefore I now turn to this special kind of narrative – scholarly texts.

EXERCISE

Exercise 7.1: deconstruction

Take a short text (or a fragment of a text) from your daily or weekly paper and analyze it using the strategies listed by Joanne Martin.

FURTHER READING

Davies, Bronwyn (1989) *Frogs and Snails and Feminist Tales*. North Sydney: Allen & Unwin.
Martin, Joanne (1990) 'Deconstructing organizational taboos: the suppression of gender conflict in organizations', *Organization Science*, 1 (4): 339–59.
Silverman, David, and Torode, Brian (1980) *The Material Word. Some Theories about Language and their Limits*. London: Routledge & Kegan Paul.

Notes

1 More on positioning in identity formation can be found in Davies and Harré (1991).
2 As the texts were translated, it would be difficult to look for the elements of the text, as Silverman and Torode did, although they did attempt it on a French text (1980: 34–5). They distinguished *pictures* (clauses, 'atomic units of meaning'), *stanzas* (grouping of clauses), and *voices* (names around which stanzas are built). It is somewhat reminiscent of Greimas' narrative programs, narrative trajectories, and actants.
3 As a part of course work during a method course held by me at Stockholm School of Economics, Fall 1994.

8

Reading Social Science

This chapter claims that all the analytical approaches discussed in previous chapters can be, and in fact have been, applied to scientific texts. It thus changes the focus from the *kind* of approach applied to the *area* to which it is applied. It argues that science is a field of practice like any other, and therefore its narratives, their production and circulation, can be studied in the same way. Misia Landau's analysis of evolution stories (Chapter 6) already announced this possibility and, although many narrative analyses focus on natural science texts (see, e.g., Mulkay, 1985; Latour, 1988), there are several that scrutinize narratives in social science texts. I will present them chronologically as this order will also reveal the developments in reflection mode that took place over time in the social sciences.

Dramatist analysis of drinking driver research

Joseph Gusfield (1976) was one of the first authors to apply rhetorical analysis to social science research. His article begins ominously: 'The Rhetoric of Research! The title imposes the obvious contradiction. Research is Science; the discovery of transmission of a true state of things. Rhetoric is Art' (1976: 16). Little did he know that the following years would be spent on dismantling this contradiction. Ricca Edmondson wrote *Rhetoric in Sociology* in 1984 and D.N. McCloskey published *The Rhetoric of Economics* in 1985. In 1987, *The Rhetoric of the Human Sciences: Language and Argument in Scholarship and Public Affairs* (edited by Nelson, Megill and McCloskey) was published, followed by

Herbert Simons' edited collection, *Rhetoric in the Human Sciences* in 1988. But in 1976 the idea of scientific-language-as-a-windowpane (science being a window to reality) dominated. Therefore, said Gusfield, an excursion to literary theory will help. He did not claim that science was literature but that treating science as literature will be productive – the very assumption of this chapter and, indeed, of this whole book.

The material Gusfield analyzed was 45 major research papers concerned with drinking and driving in Europe and the USA, and he chose one as most typical for a close reading. The analysis was divided into three parts (called acts): the literary style of science, the literary art in science, and the relevance of art in science.

In the first act, Gusfield employed Burke's dramatist analysis. Such an analysis looks for congruence – or incongruence – of five elements, known as Burke's pentad (Burke, 1945/1969): Scene (in the sense of a setting, a context, etc.), Act (in the sense of an action, a deed, or an action program), Agent (actor, actant), Agency (the means with which the Act is accomplished), and Purpose. The following are the results.

Scene

All 45 papers were published in research journals: most in medical journals, some in journals dedicated to car safety or safety in general. This setting 'establishes a claim for the paper to be taken as an authoritative fact and not as fiction or imaginative writing' (1976: 18–19).

Act

There are actually two acts which, in the terms used in this book, could be distinguished as *the act in the text* (what does the text say?) and *the act of the text* (what does the text do?). The act in the text is a causally connected narrative: (significant) numbers of drunk drivers turn out to be problem drinkers rather than social drinkers; therefore new prevention methods must be employed. Or, to put it in terms of a minimal plot:

1 Once upon a time, drunk drivers were supposed to be social drinkers.
2 New identification methods permitted recognition of drunk drivers as problem drinkers.
3 New methods of prevention of drunk driving must be found.

The act of the text is in the article's structure. It begins with setting up a challenge: the old theory of drunk driving is wrong. It continues with the description of methods used to identify problem drinkers among the drunk drivers, proceeds to the findings achieved with these methods, and ends with policy recommendations: 'This centrality of method and externality of data is the major key to the story' (p. 19).

Agent

The problem of the agent, or the voice, is not easy. On the one hand, the author of a scientific text is the reality itself, and therefore no human voice should intrude. On the other hand, the structure of the paper reveals that there is and has been an observer and a writer, and this person needs credibility and trust. This is resolved, says Gusfield, by introducing the author through his role (an organizational affiliation) and by avoiding the active voice: 'Recent reports have suggested …' (Author, Date); 'It is increasingly becoming apparent…'; 'Differences were found …' If I may complete Gusfield at this point, another technique of introducing the passive voice is often practiced, invariably with comic effects: writing about oneself in the third person: 'As Czarniawska has pointed out…'

Agency

As the result of this specific technique of representing the Agent, the main responsibility for action is displaced to Agency (yet another illustration of the convenience of the term 'actant'). In this case, it is the method.

Purpose

The purpose of the act is to convince but, due to the specific character of the act, only some techniques of persuasion are permissible. In short, pathos must be excluded to the benefit of logos (ethos always creeps in, if only in the citation procedure). The author 'means to persuade, but only by presenting an external world to the audience and allowing that external reality to do the persuading' (Gusfield, 1976: 20).

In the second act, Gusfield analyzes the use of tropes in the paper: metonymy, metaphor, myth, and archetype, whose use makes the paper close to a generic form known as a *morality play*, 'in which drinking [*sic*] driving is an arena for the expression of personal and moral character' (p. 26). In this drama, the drinking driver has been transformed from a tolerable social drinker into a stigmatized deviant. Thus, in the third act, Gusfield shows that the author of the article performed a shift in the hierarchy of main actors: what was down went up, what was up went down. The social drinkers are now not only tolerable but they are also benevolent – after all, they do not cause drunk–driving accidents. The drunk drivers turn out to be problem drinkers, not surprisingly coming from the lowest strata of the social structure. Thus, a non-emotional paper has produced quite a load of emotions – by performing theater.

Gusfield himself is well aware that all his comments could be applied to his own text, and this is why, I believe, he structures it as a three-act play. He is nevertheless convinced that a literary reflection, including self-reflection, will be useful not only to scientific texts but even to the public policies that they are supposed to inform. After all, '[i]t is this capacity to recognize the context of unexamined assumptions and accepted concepts that is among the most valuable contributions through which social science enables human beings to transcend the conventional and create new approaches and policies' (Gusfield, 1976: 32). I wish more policy-makers would read Gusfield.

The anthropologist as author

In what follows I will concentrate on the famous work by Clifford Geertz (1988), but I would like to point out that, in the same year, John Van Maanen published his *Tales of the Field*. I do not report on both in order to keep a somewhat even distribution among samples from different social sciences, but Van Maanen's book is, and has been, of great importance to all ethnographers.

Geertz begins by saying that, at the moment of his writing, it has become obvious that ethnography is not a matter of sorting strange facts into familiar categories but a kind of writing. There have been, however, hesitations as to the appropriateness of treating it as such. One such hesitation stemmed from the assumption that literary reflection is not a duty of anthropologists, who should busy themselves doing fieldwork. Another had to do with the feeling that anthropological texts, unlike literary texts, are not deserving of such attention. The third one, and recognizable to all social scientists, had to do with the suspicion that such an analysis will threaten the scientific status of these texts: 'should the literary character of anthropology be better understood, some professional myths about how it manages to persuade would be impossible to maintain' (Geertz, 1988: 3). Behind them all, says Geertz, there has been an anxiety concerning the solution of two problems: of *signature* (*author-saturated* versus *author-evacuated* texts) and of *discourse* (choice of vocabulary, rhetoric, pattern of argument). This solution had to be subordinated to the main task the anthropologists posited for themselves: creating a convincing impression of 'being there'. He decides to inspect how the great authors of anthropology, those who opted for a clear signature and a visible 'theater of language', succeeded in this task.

The first of them is Claude Lévi-Strauss, the structuralist, and the work Geertz inspects is *Tristes Tropiques*. He does it from a perspective he calls 'appreciative and unconverted' (1988: 27): he does not approve of the idea of the universal mind and is skeptical toward structuralism as an approach, but admires Lévi-Strauss as an author. He finds several books interweaved in the text of *Tristes Tropiques*. To begin with, it is a *travelogue*: 'I went here, I went there; I saw this strange thing and that; I was amazed, bored, excited, disappointed; I got boils on my behind...' (p. 33). Secondly, it is an *ethnography*: apart from the 'report from there', it has a thesis: that people's customs form into systems (here, a structuralist categorization is clearly visible). Thirdly, it is a *philosophical text* that addresses itself to the issue of the natural foundation of human society. This leads to yet another text: a *reformist tract*, based on a devastating critique of western society, which spoils the natural order in its misguided attempt to modernize. Finally, the book is a *symbolist literary text*, as has been noticed before by literary critics. The mixture, in Geertz's reading, is a myth of Anthropologist-as-seeker. In the eyes of Lévi-Strauss, empiricist Anglo-Saxon anthropology is mistaken; the impression of 'being there' is either a fraud or self-deception. Lévi-Strauss, the mythological seeker, discovers only other people's myths: the world resides in texts.

Consequently, Geertz proceeds to inspect an Anglo-Saxon author: Sir Edward Evan Evans-Pritchard whom he calls 'stylistically one of the most homogeneous writers the world has seen' (p. 49). The text he chooses is the little known 'Operations on the Akobo and Gila Rivers, 1940–41', published in a British military journal in 1973, where Evans-Pritchard describes his actions as a bush-irregular in Sudan. In Geertz's opinion, this short text displays all the traits of Evans-Pritchard's way of dealing with discourse. The metaphor Geertz uses is a 'slide-show', which could be called 'Images of Africa'. The *staccato* tone is one of the devices used to achieve an impression of complete certainty, what Geertz calls an 'of-course' discourse. The simple subject-predicate-object sentences are favored, punctuation marks are scarce, there are no foreign phrases or literary allusions: 'Everything that is said is clearly said, confidently and without fuss' (p. 61). The only (barely perceptible) trope is irony, which serves to distanciate the author from the events described in the text; in spite of this, the effect is strongly visual (hence 'slide-show').

What is the purpose of such a style (Geertz sees Evans-Pritchard as an accomplished stylist)? Evans-Pritchard was curious about how was it possible to have a cognitive order without science, a political order without the state, a spiritual order without a church – in short, a society without modern western institutions. His answer was that witchcraft, segmentary organization, and alternative ways of imagining divinity work as well. The 'of-course' tone witnesses to the sincerity of such a judgment, dis-enstranging the apparently bizarre. As Geertz puts it, Evans-Pritchard describes the Nilotes 'as not other but otherwise (sensible enough when you get to know them, but with their own way of doing things)' (p. 70). Geertz continues: 'The marvel of this rather dialectical approach to ethnography is that it validates the ethnographer's form of life at the same time as it justifies those of his subjects – and that it does one by doing the other.' Alas, this kind of device is no longer available for the ethnographers of today – of the era of 'confidence lost'.

In the case of Bronislaw Malinowski, Geertz contrasts the anthropologist's famous credo with his diary. Malinowski is known for his belief in participative observation, 'plunging into the life of the natives' as the only valuable method of fieldwork. His diary, published posthumously, caused much uneasiness, revealing the author's hypochondria, xenophobia, and a host of other non-heroic and non-scientific attitudes. To Geertz, the diary reveals much more than this array of human foibles. It shows that:

there is a lot more than native life to plunge into if one is to attempt this total immersion approach to ethnography. There is the landscape. There is the isolation. There is the local European population. There is the memory of home and what one has left. There is the sense of vocation and where one is going. And, most shakingly, there is the capriciousness of one's passions, the weakness of one's constitution, and the vagrancies of one's thoughts: that nigrescent thing, the self. It is not a question of going native ... It is a question of living a multiple life: sailing at once in several seas. (1988: 77)

If things are so complex and complicated more by the interference of the self, how to report them, then? Geertz calls Malinowski's solution an 'I-witnessing': rendering one's account credible through rendering oneself credible. This, according to Geertz, is not a psychological but a literary endeavor. In Malinowski's version, it was realized by the projection of two antithetical and therefore complementary images: of an Absolute Cosmopolite and a Complete Investigator, one standing for romance, the other for science. The first is one with the natives; the second is totally distanced from them. In fact, the oxymoron of 'participative observation' announces it quite openly. And although Malinowski's structural-functionalist theory is considered obsolete, the perplexities of the I-witnessing are very much in the center of contemporary anthropology, as Geertz's many examples show.

The fourth exemplar Geertz discusses is Ruth Benedict. Inspired by Swift and his *Gulliver's Travels*, she made the familiar culture odd and arbitrary, while the exotic one was presented as logical and obvious. Geertz calls this textual strategy 'us/not-us' and points out that, partly because she was a woman, and women are not supposed to be ironic, Benedict's irony sometimes went unappreciated (as compared to that of Ervin Goffman, for example). A juxtaposition of the familiar and of the exotic is obviously a sophisticated literary strategy, but it is prone to produce disconcert, not least because of its comic effect. According to Geertz, the two works that reached mass popularity – *Patterns of Culture* and *The Chrysanthemum and the Sword* – did so because Benedict managed to suppress their humorous aspect, presenting herself as utterly sincere. He emphasizes that Benedict's accomplishment was not her fieldwork, of which there was little, and not her systematic theorizing, 'in which she was scarcely interested' (p. 108), but her 'distinctive sort of redescription: the sort that startles' (p. 112).

There are at least two reasons why Geertz's musing about anthropological writing is relevant to all social sciences. One is that anthropology has become fashionable, not as before as a postcard from an exotic land, but as a way of 'being here', to quote Geertz again. Anthropologists came back home, not least as the result of the changed political landscape, and infected the rest of us with their methods and their doubts. Secondly, but also as a result of it, one premise became common to all social sciences: '[t]he gap between engaging others where they are and representing them when they aren't, always immense but not much noticed, has suddenly become extremely visible' (p. 130). The Other is here, is literate, and has a voice – no wonder that the theory of representation is in crisis.

The lessons from reading Geertz reading other authors are many, but one is especially poignant: 'the burden of authorship cannot be evaded, however heavy it may have grown; there is no possibility of displacing it onto "method", "language", or ... "the people themselves" redescribed ... as co-authors' (p. 140).

Storytelling in economics

It can be pointed out that anthropology and its offspring, ethnography, even at their most 'scientific', were always closer to *belles lettres* than were other social sciences. In this case, a good example to consider will be economics – rarely suspected of such a propinquity. Deirdre McCloskey has thoroughly analyzed the rhetoric of economics (1985; 1994) but she has also devoted some attention specifically to the role of narratives in economics (1990a; 1990b).

'Economists are tellers of stories and makers of poems, and from recognizing this we can know better what economists do' (1990b: 5). Metaphors (models) and stories (narratives) seem to be two competing but also complementary modes of knowing. A metaphor can bring a point to a story while a story can exemplify a metaphor. In the sciences, metaphors are typical of physics and stories of biology. Economics, claims McCloskey, presents a balanced mixture of both. The two work best in specific areas: metaphors in predictions, simulations and counterfactuals, and stories in explaining something that actually happened. It can be seen when their areas of expertise cross: a business cycle is a story, describing the past. When applied as a model and therefore to a prediction of the future, it dies of its own contradiction: if business cycles could be predicted they would not happen (a conclusion worth considering in the context of the failure of the new economy).

Looking at economics as a storytelling business, claims McCloskey, helps us understand why economists disagree, without thus necessarily being 'bad economists'. Within the traditional perspective on economic texts as transparent (that is, economic writing as 'putting in script theoretical premises and empirical findings'), the disagreements are inexplicable, unless by ill will. In the same vein, but with some admission of an authorial effort, it is traditionally assumed that disagreements are misunderstandings arising from the fact that the writer does not have enough time and space (for example, in a paper format) to explicate things properly. But, says McCloskey, even if writers did have enough time and space, the readers wouldn't. There is a whole plethora of texts vying for attention, and economic texts must fight for it like all others. Finally, another traditional explanation of disagreements is a suspicion that the reader is unable to take the point of view demanded by the author, this time because of intellectual limitations. This suspicion of the readers, promises McCloskey, will vanish when the economic authors understand that economics, and schools within economics, are separate languages, or at least dialects, which to many a reader read like texts in a foreign language.

McCloskey therefore launches on reading economics as storytelling embellished with metaphors. She points out that a structuralist reading is not an option as '[e]conomics is already structural' (1990b: 13). The 'functions' in economic texts will never arrive at Propp's number of 31; there is entry, exit, price setting, orders within a firm, purchase, sale, valuation, and not many more. 'Propp … found seven characters … David Ricardo in his economic tales got along with three' (1990b: 14). The economic stories also show a preference for a plot that is ending-embedded, as Jean Matter Mandler called it (see Chapter 6): 'Go all the way to the third act.' (1990b: 14). The definition of the plot, too, is as designed for economics – the transformation of equilibrium into disequilibrium and into a subsequent equilibrium:

> Poland was poor, then it adopted capitalism, then as a result it became rich.

> The money supply increased this year; then, as a result, productivity last year rose and the business cycle three decades ago peaked. (McCloskey, 1990a: 26)

In terms of genre analysis, there are two analyses that are most common. Theoretical work in economics is similar to the literary genre of fantasy; the empirical work is like a realistic novel.

McCloskey quotes many examples to corroborate her analysis, of which I will quote two. One concerns the literary text that introduced and popularized the main concept of classical economics, the *Homo economicus*. The other concerns a contemporary text by an economist, known and quoted widely in other social sciences and in the popular press.

The first text is Daniel Defoe's *Robinson Crusoe*.[1] Although the idea of *Homo economicus* came to economics officially, as it were, at the end of the nineteenth century as an analogy with molecules, Defoe's text already presents it in full. Robinson Crusoe perceives the world as a series of opportunities to be chosen from according to their costs. McCloskey points out that the notion of 'opportunity costs' was fully developed by Austrian economists in the 1870s but seemed to be always obvious to poets and, later, to novelists. Robinson Crusoe's situation is a quintessence of scarcity – another notion known earlier in literature than in economics:

> Each time Crusoe or any *homo economicus* faces a choice he draws up a balance sheet in his head … but more commonly he uses commercial metaphors, especially those of accounting … This is the rational way to proceed – understanding 'rational' to mean merely a sensible adjustment of what you can to what you want. So the rational person is a calculator, like Crusoe, making rough and ready choices about what to put next on the boat. … The details of style throughout the book contribute to the force of scarcity – a contrast to the stories of shipwrecks in the *Odyssey* or the *Aeneid*, over which hover intervening gods willing to perform miracles of abundance. (McCloskey, 1990a: 145)

McCloskey analyzes several works of economic historians (Gershenkron, Fogel) to show how they constructed their stories, but also offers an interesting reading of Lester Thurow's *The Zero-sum Solution: Building a World-class American Economy* (1985) as an example of an uneasy cooperation between stories and metaphors. The book was written in the years of the 'Japanese miracle' and is addressed to the ways the USA should cope with it.

Three metaphors govern Thurow's story: the 'international zero-sum game', the 'domestic problem', which damages US performance in the game, and 'we' who need to cope with the problem. Income and wealth need to be dredged from non-Americans and 'every competitive game has its losers'. 'For a society which loves team sports ... it is surprising that Americans won't recognize the same reality in the far more important international economics game' (McCloskey, 1990a: 156). When less benevolent, Thurow changes the competitive sport metaphor to a war metaphor, seeing foreign trade as the economic equivalent of war.

Sport metaphors and even war metaphors are as old as modern economics, points out McCloskey: in the late nineteenth century, British journalists wrote about the 'American threat' and the 'German menace'. US journalists use them all the time. The problem with Thurow's metaphors, however, is that they do not fit his story.

The topic of his story is the exchange of goods and services: Japanese cars for US timber, German steel tubes for Soviet natural gas. Such an exchange is in metaphorical tune with Adam Smith's idea of voluntary trade: everyone wins – this is why they continue to trade.

The zero-sum game metaphor concerns only one part of trade: the selling side. This is an obvious perspective for a businessperson from Massachusetts but it should not be, points out McCloskey, for an economist. An economist, even from Massachusetts, should be looking wider. After all, economists claim to see around and underneath the economy ('underneath it all' being a favorite economic turn of phrase), and to account for it from the societal point of view.

Another metaphor (label?) that needs unpicking is the mysterious 'we'. Who is it, in Thurow's account? 'We Americans'? Not necessarily, points out McCloskey:

> problems have solutions, called 'policies', which 'we must adopt'. It is not hard to guess who the Solver is: I'm from the Government, and I'm here to solve your problem ... Do economists really know enough that planning for research and development, ... should be handed over to a MIT-ish organization? (1990a: 158)

And what is the 'domestic problem' that prevents the USA from winning the zero-sum game? It is the 'productivity problem', and McCloskey has quite a lot to say about this:

> 'The Productivity Problem' in recent American history is not a figment ... But in any case productivity has nothing to do with international competitiveness and the balance

of payment. As your local economist will be glad to make clear, the pattern of trade depends on comparative advantage, not absolute advantage ... The overall level of productivity has no effect on America's trade balance. None. And the trade balance is not a measure of excellence. None. The two having nothing to do with each other. We could achieve an enormous and positive trade balance tomorrow with no pursuit of excellence by forbidding imports. Americans want to trade with Tatsuro, and it makes them better off to do so: that is all. (1990a: 160–1)

Does it mean that Lester Thurow is a bad storyteller and unskillful metaphor user? To the contrary: it is the fact that he is a skillful storyteller that prevents his readers from inspecting his metaphors and his stories. Not only does he use taken-for-granted metaphors but he also builds legitimacy for its story in analogy. His story is a parallel to the one well known, the one about late Victorian Britain: 'in the sunset of hegemony, Britain basked complacently while others hustled' (McCloskey, 1990a: 158). As we have seen in the studies of Mandler (1984) and Davies (1989), readers easily recognize familiar narratives and unproblematically accept, and even reconstruct, their structure. So it is in a truly deconstructivist vein that McCloskey asks her final questions:

And why would one wish American hegemony to be fastened on the world forever? Is it God's plan that the United States of America should ever after be Top Nation? Why should we wish relative poverty in perpetuity on our Chinese and Latin American friends? Is this what economic ethics leads us to? (1990a: 159)

Thurow's book was written in 1985; McCloskey's close reading of it in 1990. Since then, Japan ceased to be a menace. In 2002, President Bush was more than ever dedicated to the zero-sum game (he might even take McCloskey's advice and forbid imports altogether), but the 2001 winner of the Bank of Sweden's prize in the name of Alfred Nobel, Joseph E. Stiglitz, uses a rhetoric very different from Thurow's:

Global leadership requires not only being against something; it requires being for something. We have an alliance against terrorism. We should also have an alliance for more global justice and a better global environment. Globalization has made us more interdependent, and this interdependence makes it necessary to undertake global collective action. (2002: 28)[2]

Perhaps McCloskey's close reading of economists' texts has contributed to a legitimation of such alternative rhetoric in the economic sciences.

It has been pointed out to McCloskey that 'writing well' is uneconomical, that too much awareness of one's stories and metaphors, too much effort put into self-reflection and writing itself, does not pay – in terms of academic career. Her answer is, again, couched in ethical terms:

It is unethical to write badly when at small cost you can do better, and it is especially unethical to cultivate obscurity to get some material benefit ... I would say, with Socrates in the *Gorgias*, that it is better to suffer evil (lack of promotion) than to perpetrate it (writing in the Official Style for selfish advantage). (McCloskey, 2000: 138–9)

There are two vices in McCloskey's 'book of writing': writing well so as to deceive the readers (as in Thurow's case), and writing badly so as to deceive the judges (obfuscation). Tough requirements, but then the stakes of economics are high.

Leadership as seduction: deconstructing social science theory

The last example of the analysis of social science texts concerns an organiza-tion theory text, but on a topic that is of interest to many social sciences: leadership. Marta B. Calás and Linda Smircich, following the suggestion of Baudrillard, juxtaposed the notions of leadership and seduction:

> They wanted us to believe that everything is production. The leitmotiv of world trans-formation, the play of productive forces is to regulate the flow of things. Seduction is merely an immoral, frivolous, superficial and superfluous process: one within the realm of signs and appearances; one that is devoted to pleasure and to the usufruct of useless bodies. What if everything, contrary to appearances – in fact according to the secret rule of appearances – operated by the [principle of] seduction? (Baudrillard, cited in Calás and Smircich, 1991: 567)

What if leadership is a seduction? Calás and Smircich used three poststruc-turalist approaches: Foucault's genealogy, Derrida's deconstruction, and feminist poststructuralism to re-read four classics of organization theory: Chester Barnard's *The Functions of the Executive* (1938), Douglas McGregor's *The Human Side of the Enterprise* (1960), Henry Mintzberg's *The Nature of Managerial Work* (1973), and Thomas J. Peters and Robert H. Waterman's *In Search of Excellence* (1982). These texts are important because they were written for the audience of practitioners (managers) but have also had a strong impact on the academic community.

As I have already quoted examples of poststructuralist and deconstructivist reading, I shall focus on Calás and Smircich's use of Foucault's genealogy. As is now well known, Foucault used historical analysis to show how various inter-twined power structures produce, and are reproduced by, a network of prac-tices and discourses that is usually called *knowledge*.[3] Calás and Smircich's ambition is to show how all the consecutive work legitimizes itself by announcing change and transformation of the insights of their predecessor, while at the same time reproducing and maintaining the same network of knowledge-about-leadership production.

Calás and Smircich began with contrasting the dictionary definitions of 'leadership' and 'seduction'. They turn out very close, as 'to seduce' is 'to lead away' (or 'astray'). Seduction is leadership gone wrong, whereas leadership seems to be a seduction gone right. Also, the words 'seductor' or 'seducer' are deemed obsolete: 'seductress' is the only contemporary form. Enriched by these etymological insights, Calás and Smircich proceed with their genealogy.

The texts they choose cover a period of almost 50 years of theorizing about organizations, a period that, according to Calás and Smircich and contrary to what the authors themselves say, shows practically no change. The text traces a circle of seduction – while practices and discourses of leadership change, they preserve the same power/knowledge relationships.

In Barnard's text, the motive of seduction is present by its absence, by its silence. Many a time the text comes close to this dangerous border ('Leadership, of course, often is wrong, and often fails' – Barnard, cited in Calás and Smircich, 1991: 576), dangerous to the maintenance of social structure such as an organization, and the succession of leadership. Barnard's language of morality used to describe the leader

> (faith, sacrifice, abstention, reverence) calls to mind images of a priest (usually called 'Father') – an individual of superior determination, whose endurance and courage are more inferred from what he avoids (*does not* do): succumbing to temptation, and engaging in sexual intercourse. Seduction, as seduction, is inimical to orderly relations of men/human life. (p. 577)

McGregor's book was hailed as an introduction of humanistic psychology into the managerial discourse. Addressed to the top managers of US corporations in the 1960s, it attempts to answer a question: who can be a leader? The book claims a separation from Barnard's idea of a lonely executive in his room on the top floor: the leadership postulated by McGregor is egalitarian, relational, and situational. Yet according to Calás and Smircich, McGregor only develops and embellishes Barnard's homosocial, 'fatherly' reasoning.

McGregor's innovation is known as replacing 'theory X' (traditional management theory à la Taylor and Barnard) with a 'theory Y' (human relations theory). Why, ask Calás and Smircich, those letters? Why not 'theories A and B' or 'A and Z'? They point out that it was exactly at that time that women became defined as having two X chromosomes, while men were defined as 'XY'. McGregor's can therefore be read, deconstructively but interestingly, as an attempt to move from an XY world to a sheer YY world: a homosocial order. Alternatively, and it is my alternative, it could be seen as presenting the earlier theories as 'too feminine' (seductive) to be replaced by more masculine (XY).

Henry Mintzberg's work was an elaboration of his doctoral dissertation, reporting his study that consisted of observing managers in their everyday work. *The Nature of Managerial Work* is a stylized version of the dissertation and attempts to answer the question: what do managers do? Calás and Smircich observe that in the 13 years that passed between the two books, McGregor's relationship-oriented leader has been transformed into Mintzberg's 'solitary and narcissistic, but omnipotent, leader with no patience for anything but the most direct encounter...' (1991: 586–7).

In order to understand this transformation, Calás and Smircich widen their genealogy to include other texts from the same period: the issue of growing narcissism during those 13 years was becoming the central issue in US reflective literature. Philip Slater has written about it in his *Footholds* (1977), and Christopher Lasch's *The Culture of Narcissism* became a bestseller in 1979. Mintzberg's narcissistic leader was, therefore, a good representative of his time. Narcissism is not limited to men, though; women are perfectly capable of narcissist conduct. Quoting Karen Horney, Calás and Smircich claim, however, that narcissistic – and seductive – activities in adult age differ between men and women. Men define their self-esteem and affirm their power through devaluing women, in this way reasserting the narcissistic belief about their superior position in society. Feminine seductiveness, on the other hand, is a conversion of fear into desirability, a way of promoting a submissive identity in order to avoid aggression. Therefore, 'feminine narcissistic activities will maintain – through submission or cloning – the homosocial order' (1991: 588):

> Mintzberg's leader – compulsively masculine in its narcissistic seduction – plays on the conditions of modern Western society. Under Mintzberg's leader, those for whom compulsive masculinity is not a value will still submit to its ruling. Lacking other options within the system, they will perpetuate the conditions they may be wishing to escape. (Calás and Smircich, 1991: 589)

Just after the article by Calás and Smircich, *Organization Studies* published 'A letter to Marta Calás and Linda Smircich' by Henry Mintzberg. Bitterly ironic, it also revealed a deeply hurt author. As Gusfield (1976) has already pointed out, any 'close reading' makes the reader 'a smartass' and the writer a dupe. But Mintzberg also makes an important point: we – the academic writers – have also set out to seduce the readers 'in a way that puts almost all mortal leaders to shame' (Mintzberg, 1991: 602).

Some authors solve this difficulty by offering a reflection on their own texts, preempting the possible close readings. But no author can preempt all the readings, and a reflection over a reflection quickly loses its attractiveness, as brilliantly demonstrated in Malcolm Ashmore's book *The Reflexive Thesis* (1989).

Back to leadership: Calás and Smircich see Peters and Waterman's bestseller as closing the circle of seduction. Peters and Waterman confess at the outset that they assumed the importance of leadership to be exaggerated: in other words, all their predecessors were wrong. It turned out, however, that with every excellent company was associated a strong leader (or two). The corporate world of the 1980s contained many women, but the basic relationships were not changed, although in the text 'he or she' and 'his or her' were duly introduced. When it comes to defining the leader of the 1980s, Peters and

Waterman go back to basics – a 'transformational leader'. This leader is a male, at least grammatically, and is busy with things that Barnard would have approved of: raising his subordinates to higher levels of motivation and morality (and being raised by them, so that McGregor gets his due), and exercising leadership that might be called 'elevating, mobilizing, inspiring, exalting, uplifting, exhorting, evangelizing' (cited in Calás and Smircich, 1991: 592).

At the time of writing, seductive leadership took another beating after a series of frauds, excessive remunerations, etc. Henry Mintzberg (1999) writes about 'managing quietly', clearly irritated with narcissistic leaders. Will the circle of seduction recreate itself once again?

Narratives from one's own backyard

It can be observed that the narratives from one's own practice are analyzed like all others, possibly with more bravado (after all, the analyst is on safe ground, at least epistemologically if not always politically) but also with special care due to the fact that the narrators cannot be anonymized. Many different options are open beyond those I have presented here. There are works and anthologies that concentrate on analysis of a specific discipline: psychology (Ellen Herman, 1995), anthropology (Clifford and Marcus, 1986), sociology (Richard Harvey Brown, 1977; Ricca Edmondson, 1984), social studies of science and technology (Ashmore, 1989), management and organization (Czarniawska, 1999a; Rhodes, 2001). There are works and anthologies that present an array of analyses of social or, as they are sometimes called, human sciences (Nelson et al., 1987; R.H. Brown, 1989; 1995; 1998; Simons, 1989; 1990; Agger, 1990; Nash, 1990). There exist comparisons between fiction and social science (e.g., Paola Cappetti, 1993). The moment of surprise and disconcert at attempting such narrative analysis to social sciences has passed; the opportunities for reflecting and learning have barely opened.

EXERCISE

Exercise 8.1: social science text analysis

Take three texts from your discipline dealing with the same topic. Compare them for differences and similarities. Then choose an approach that seems to be most fruitful (rhetorical analysis, genealogy, deconstruction, or a close reading using a combination of several approaches) and attempt a comparative analysis of the three.

FURTHER READING

Brown, Richard Harvey (1998) *Toward a Democratic Science. Scientific Narration and Civic Communication.* New Haven, CT: Yale University Press.
Nash, Cristopher (ed.) (1990) *Narrative in Culture. The Uses of Storytelling in the Sciences, Philosophy and Literature.* London: Routledge.
Nelson, John S., Megill, Allan, and McCloskey, D.N. (eds) *The Rhetoric of Human Sciences.* Madison, WI: University of Wisconsin Press.

Notes

1   This is not a fancy reading by an exaggeratingly literary mind. Defoe was a journalist and a pamphletist, famous for his *Giving Alms No Charity and Employing the Poor A Grievance to the Nation*, published in 1704 (Karl Polanyi, 1944).
2   Although the notion of US hegemony remains unquestioned.
3   See Gavin Kendall and Gary Wickham's *Using Foucault's Methods* (1998).

9

Writing Social Science

As mentioned in Chapter 2, there are three elements to a narrative: chronicle, mimesis, and plot. As chronicle is usually not a problem in scientific writing, I will leave it aside and concentrate on mimesis and plot.[1]

Mimesis, or how to represent the world

In this book, the notion of mimesis, as representation of the world in a text, is related to two elements of 'the world': the field of theory and the field of practice under study. In other words, I will make no big difference between writing a literature review and writing up a fieldwork.[2] Both need to re-present scientific literature or inscriptions of everyday life, and both need to emplot their representations.

Problems with re-presentation

A commonsense answer to a question: 'how to represent?' is: faithfully. Reality should be re-created in the text. A scientific text should reflect what it describes, hopefully in a one-to-one correspondence. This should not be any problem as 'facts speak for themselves', and texts can be rendered loyally to the intentions of the authors.

That this is possible at all was questioned by Impressionists in art and, by among others, Jorge Luis Borges in literature,[3] and finally in human sciences.[4] The following problems emerged:

- The incompatibility of worlds and words (Rorty, 1980; 1989): how can words be compared to that which they (purportedly) describe? A one-to-one correspondence is impossible if media are different.[5] It is therefore sensible to think of representation of an object as involving *production* of another object 'which is intentionally related to the first by a certain coding convention which determines what counts as similar in the right way' (Van Fraassen and Sigman, 1993: 74). Representation does not reflect; it creates.
- The politics of representation (Latour, 1999): considering that there are always competing versions of the world in circulation, who, and by what criteria, has the right to judge them? This second problem is already a search for a solution to the first one: if facts do not speak for themselves, who will speak on their behalf? How do conventions of coding arise? Who has the right to judge what is 'the right way'?

As these are complex queries, let me begin from the opposite end and ask: what is the purpose of skillful mimesis in a social science monograph? The common (academic) sense answer is: in the case of field material, *to make readers feel as if they were there, in the field*; in case of a literature review, *to make readers feel as if they read the literature themselves*. How to achieve these effects, if facts refuse to speak for themselves and a truly faithful rendering of somebody else's text is plagiarism? There can be no normative answer to this question, only descriptive: I can tell the readers how authors try to achieve this effect.

Words cannot be compared to non-words, only to other words. This means that, as Hayden White (1999) put it, all descriptions of historical objects (and social objects are historical) are necessarily *figurative*. In order to evoke in readers an image of something they have not seen, this image must be connected to something they have already seen, and *tropes* – figures of speech – are the linguistic means to achieve just this effect. The word *metaphor* which, in Greek, means a transport from one place to another, means exactly that in authorial practice: the reader is moved from 'here' to 'there', be it another physical setting or another book. Also, not for nothing are tropes *figures* of speech: they are the means to visualize, 'to paint with words'.

White speaks of 'figural realism' which, as I read it, is identical to what Richard H. Brown called 'symbolic realism' (1977), with one important difference. While Brown considered symbolic realism as *a kind of* realism, counterpoised to, for example, scientific realism, White points out that *all* realism *is* necessarily symbolic – that is, figurative. Realism differs from other literary styles by the preference for certain tropes and not others (understatement rather than overstatement, to take an obvious example). Nevertheless, the question still remains: how to produce a realistic representation?

The setting

While mimesis is a task to be fulfilled throughout the thesis, it is in the description of the setting that it comes to the fore. Unfortunately, the setting description tends to be the least attractive part of all theses, which pick up the pace when it comes to presentation of what has happened, rather than at the stage when it must be said 'what it looked like'. It seems that many authors become excessively conscious of a referential contract: 'I am writing to instruct, not to entertain, and you can go and check that my description is correct, if you wish.' The problem is, as all educators know, that the 'fictional' and the 'referential' contracts are never separate; they only take on a different priority in different texts. In other words, it is difficult, if not impossible, to instruct without pleasing, or entertaining, or moving, the readers.

The setting, as the term indicates, describes the context of the phenomenon under scrutiny – in spatiotemporal terms. A literary context is other theories of the same or of similar phenomena, and it is important to locate them in their proper time and place. There are no universal theories; there are only theories with universalistic claims. They all come from a certain place at a certain time – see my attempts to contextualize Bittner's text in Chapter 5. Common malpractices are disregarding the date of the original publication (so that the writings of Max Weber seem to be under the influence of the lessons he has learned from, let's say, James G. March and Herbert Simon), or the implicit assumption that the insights 'made in the USA' are valid all over the world. Each text, even that of a classic, is like a letter – written in response to another text and with a hope of provoking an answer. It is not always easy to uncover the network of correspondents but acknowledgments and introductions are a good place to look for the clues. Also, sometimes a de-contextualization is an enriching move, but it must be preceded by a contextualization.

These difficulties do not abate when it comes to a description of the setting of a field study. Even here the context is both spatial and temporal. Although the two can be presented jointly, as they are two aspects of the same description, I shall separate them for explication's sake.

In both cases, there are two alternative strategies, which in the case of temporal description can be called 'feedforward' and 'feedback'. In the event of a feedforward strategy, a history of the phenomenon is presented ('the story so far'). Sometimes a mere chronicle will do; if a complete history (written by somebody else) is quoted, it is important to pay attention to the work of emplotment so as not to buy a ready-made plot. The choice of the beginning is very important, as explained in Chapter 2.

The choice of a feedback strategy means that the emphasis is on the description of 'here and now'. The narrative reverses in time in a selective fashion – only that which will have relevance for the future plot needs to be included. Such selectivity is more difficult in a forward movement where a chronicle needs to be somewhat complete in order to be understandable, although the relevance is always pertinent.

The two analogous strategies in describing the spatial dimension can be called, in photographic terms, 'zooming in' and 'zooming out'. The first move is from space to place: from describing a large context (a country, an industry, a global economy) to the concrete field under study, or even a site ('a school in a suburb of a big city'). The second move performs an opposite operation: from a detailed description of a concrete place, it telescopes (again, selectively) to the whole world if the need be.

Paul Atkinson, in his *The Ethnographic Imagination* (1990), gives many examples of the ethnographers' descriptions of their settings, and calls attention to a rhetorical figure called *hypothyposis*: 'the use of a highly graphic passage of descriptive writing, which portrays a scene or action in a vivid and arresting manner' (p. 71). In this way, he claims, an author establishes a narrative contract with a reader of a type I would call a hybrid of fictional and referential contracts: 'suspend your disbelief, and let me instruct you!'

One impressive way of combining all the four moves and thus creating an incentive – nay, an urge – to read further is Mike Davis' Prologue to his *City of Quartz: Excavating the Future in Los Angeles* (1990). Appropriately titled 'The view from futures past', it begins in a zoom-in, feedback mode. The author – or anybody in his place – is standing 'on the ruins of [Los Angeles'] alternative future ... the foundations of the General Assembly Hall of the Socialist city of Llano del Rio – Open Shop Los Angeles's utopian antipode...' (p. 3). Standing there, one can see the whole of Los Angeles County and look into the past. While the lens of the camera zooms out, the time goes back to 1914 – because this is when the story of the Llano utopia starts. The place determines the beginning of the story. Now the time starts moving forward, arriving at 1990, when infamous city violence put the final end to the myth of a 'desert sanctuary'.

But this forward move traces only one history – that of the settlers and their dreams. The time machine goes back again to the same point and goes forward once more, following the trail of politicians, planners, and developers. At this point the focus changes to 'here and now', now properly contextualized. It is time for a hypothyposis:

> On May Day 1990 ... I returned to the ruins of Llano del Rio to see if the walls would talk to me. Instead I found the Socialist City reinhabited by two twenty-year-old building laborers from El Salvador, camped out in the ruins of the old dairy and eager to talk to me in our mutually broken tongues. (1990: 12)

The stage is set: the readers know that the action will take place in Los Angeles County in 1990, against the background of another place – a Utopia that never came into existence – and another time (the period 1914–90). Now, who will tell the story?

Voices

While choosing the descriptive devices and strategies is a matter of skill or art, this other problem is more political in character. As the map must not be the same as the territory, it is necessary to silence some of the voices that form the polyphony of the world and to give some more space than others.

Here the parallel between dealing with a field of theory and a field of practice is very clear. The problem is common: whom to include, whom to exclude, and who deserves which type of attention? In the field of theory we have a set of conventions to aid the writer, and a set of practices, more or less recommendable.[6]

In brief, there are two main ways of dealing with other authors' texts. One is *exegetic* – that is, aiming at an explanation or a critical interpretation of a text. In this mode the other author's text is focused on: as a model or as an object of criticism. The main thing is then to re-present the other text as well as possible (that is, choosing appropriate tropes to connect the monograph to the text it analyzes) and then take a stance: admiring, apologetic, critical, a 'step beyond'.

The other, much more common in practice but rarely mentioned in prudish how-to-write-science books, is an *inspired* mode (Rorty, 1992, contrasts it with 'methodical' reading), very close to de Certeau's (1984/1988) idea of reading as *poaching*. In this mode, the other's text is re-contextualized for the purposes of the monograph. The author borrows (acknowledging the loan) notions and terms coined by others to use them in the context of the monograph.

The observation that the inspired mode of using other people's texts is more frequent than the exegetic is not a proof of lax customs in academe: unless exegesis is the topic of a monograph, the inspired mode is much more relevant to the task at hand.

What, however, about the field of practice, with its infinite multiplicity of voices and vocabularies, structured by power relations that include the social science writer?[7] The difficulty of representing the multiple voices in field studies[8] was perhaps most sharply focused on in anthropology. After decades of all-knowing anthropological texts that explained the 'native ways of being' to the 'more developed civilization', a wave of political and ethical doubts pervaded the discipline (best summarized in the volumes edited by Clifford and Marcus, 1986, and Marcus and Fischer, 1986). Many contributors to these volumes opted for a different, polyphonic ethnography, in which people could speak in their own voices, which led to much discussion about whether it was in fact possible.

It is worth recalling that these anthropologists took inspiration from Mikhail Bakhtin (1981), who had in mind not a polyphony in which many people are speaking but something called *heteroglossia* or 'variegated speech'. This is an *authorial strategy* consisting of the fact that the author speaks different languages (dialects, slangs, etc.) in the text. There is no need for the illusion that 'these people' talk for themselves; indeed they do not. No reader suspects that the four narrators in Iain Pears' novel (see Chapter 5) are speaking 'themselves'. But the author pays them a compliment by making the reader clearly aware of the fact that different languages, dialects, idiolects (personal languages) *are* being spoken within one and the same linguistic tradition.

From this perspective it is easier to approach a suggestion coming from the sociology of science and technology: of meeting the duty of representation by giving voice even to non-humans (Woolgar, 1988; Latour, 1992). Latour (1996) put this suggestion into practice in his study I discuss at more length in the next section, where 'Aramis' (an automated train system) got a voice of his (?) own. At a certain point in this story, Master and Pupil (who study Aramis' 'life') have a heated exchange on the sensibility of such a move: 'Do you think I don't know,' barks the Master at the doubting Pupil, 'that giving Aramis a voice is but an anthropomorphization, creating a puppet with a voice?' (p. 59).

Thus social science ends up with a staged conversation in which the goal of political representation must live side by side with the awareness that we are performing an act of ventriloquism. This amounts to giving up the ambition of speaking on behalf of the Other in any literal sense, the ambition to be 'a tribune for the unheard, a representer of the unseen, a kenner of the misconstrued' (Geertz, 1988: 133). But the fictiveness of this polyphony, once revealed, relieves social scientists from the criticism of silencing the voices. Social scientists do most harm when they impose their interpretations on what they claim are 'authentic voices from the field'. If rendering these voices is the purpose, the way to go about it is to quit social science (silence one's own voice) and to engage in the political activity of creating speaking platforms for those who are not heard.

Mimesis is therefore not an easy matter but not the last problem to tackle when writing a monograph. It lies in the rhetorical tradition to differentiate between mimesis (a description) and emplotment (an arrangement). But this differentiation makes only an analytical sense: it is obvious that each description must be arranged. This arrangement can be coherent with the arrangement of the whole text, or incoherent with it. In other words, mimesis can corroborate the plot or oppose it. Although it is possible to think of a mimesis opposing the plot and therefore contributing to some kind of a meta-plot, it is safe to assume that, in a social science monograph, an attempt at coherence is still a virtue. Additionally, as I have pointed out in Chapter 6, the mode of description justifies the plot (princes do not marry dirty princesses). I will suggest further that description should be subordinated to the requirements of the plot, not least in its volume: the descriptive material that is not needed in this function can be saved in an appendix. From all this it is obvious that, in my view, emplotment is the crucial part of writing a social science monograph – and the most difficult.

Plot, or how to theorize

Emplotment (a term introduced by Hayden White, 1973, who ventured to say that historians do not *find* plot in history but *put it in* themselves) means introducing structure that allows making sense of the events reported. Traditionally, it responds to a question: 'why?' – where, in a positivist view, the answer should be formulated in terms of causal laws; in a romantic view, in terms of motives; in post-positivist, post-romantic discourse (Brown, 1989), it assumes the form of showing 'how come?' where laws of nature, human intentions and random events form a hybrid mixture.

Inherited structures

The easiest way of introducing a structure is by means of chronology, or what Mandler Matter called a temporal connection (Chapter 6). Still, there are several types of chronologies that might be used. Let us look at a classic form of a thesis (a formal oration in Greek rhetoric):

1 Exordium: catches the audience's interest while introducing the subject.
2 Narration: sets forth the facts.
3 Proposition (or Division): sets forth points stipulated and points to be contested (states the case).
4 Proof: sets forth the arguments in support of the case.
5 Refutation: refutes opponents' arguments.
6 Peroration: sums up arguments and stirs audience. (Lanham, 1991)

This is an interesting example of how a meaningful structure becomes mechanical and a theory becomes pure chronology. The structure looks as it does because it was considered to work best (in the sense of doing persuasion work); in time, however, it became simply a chronology of a speech. I am quoting it partly to show how close it is to what is considered a conventional structure of a thesis, but also how meaningful persuasive devices can become mechanical by the fact that they are often repeated.

The following is a traditional structure of a thesis, shared by an article and a monograph alike (although an article has to cramp it into a much shorter space and the reader has to 'unstuff' it, like a big file that arrives 'zipped'):

1 Problem/Issue/Aims (Exordium)
2 Literature Review
3 Hypotheses (Proposition)
4 Method
5 Results (Narration)
6 Discussion (Proof)
7 Conclusion (Peroration)

The similarity is obvious, and it is no coincidence: the structure of a thesis has developed from the structure of an oration. But a thesis, in Ricoeur's terms, is a written, not a spoken discourse (the traditional structure is worth remembering when preparing an overhead presentation of a thesis!). A contemporary thesis is grounded in forensic rhetoric but has some addition of a deliberative rhetoric: thus a 'Literature Review'. What was written before is important in another way than previous precedents are important in court. The truly modern addition is the 'Method': positivism's contribution to classical rhetoric.

Not all monographs comply with this structure. It can be called a structure of a deductive thesis. An inductive thesis, let us say a thesis written in the spirit of the grounded theory approach (Glaser and Strauss, 1967), might look as follows:

1   There is something strange going on in the world... (Exordium).
2   Has somebody else explained it? (Literature review). If not:
3   I'd better go and learn more about it. But how? (Method).
4   Now that I have understood it, I will try to explain it to others. So, let me tell you a story ... (Narration).
5   Now, what does it remind me of? Is there somebody else who thinks similarly? (Proof).
6   This is the end (and the point) of my story (Peroration).

Clearly another variation of both classical oration plus the modern addenda. Like their classical predecessors, these structures hope for the persuasion effect. Like their classical predecessors, however, they also follow chronology – not of the oration, but of research itself.

This kind of temporal structuring produces as many problems as it solves. First of all, novices in the craft of research (Booth et al., 1995) often suffer from its insincerity. It is well known that research seldom goes as planned. What to do? Report all moves back and forth, hesitations, and mistakes? This can be turned into an art, but most often it is not. Lie, therefore, and suffer?

This problem (fact or fiction of research?) is nevertheless secondary. The main question is still the classic one: will it persuade? And although it is not a question that can ever be answered once and for all, the suggestion can be made that this kind of mechanical structuring is usually inferior to a successful emplotment. What is, then, a successful emplotment? I suggest that plot can be fruitfully considered to be the work's theory, which can then serve to structure a monograph substantially rather than formally.

Plots

Aristotle already differentiated between a simple story ('a narrative of events arranged in their time sequence') and a plot that arranges them according to a sense of causality (*Encyclopaedia Britannica*, 1989: 523).

As mentioned in Chapter 1, Donald Polkinghorne (1987) dedicated much attention to the role of the plot and its possible uses in the human sciences: 'The plot functions to transform a chronicle or listing of events into a schematic whole by highlighting and recognizing the contribution that certain events make to the development of the whole' (pp. 18–19). But not only that: a plot can weave into the story the historical and social context, information about physical laws, and thoughts and feelings reported by people. 'A plot has the capacity to articulate and consolidate complex threads of multiple activities by means of the overlay of subplots' (p. 19). This is an important property from the point of view of social scientists, faced often with the fact that, as many things happen simultaneously, a simple chronology is not sufficient to tell a story.

Consequently, most social science texts – but also novels, for that matter – contain more than one plot, which must be connected to one another. Such a combination of plots is usually achieved, says Todorov (1971/1977), by one of two strategies: *linking* (coordination), i.e. adding simple plots to one another so they fit, and *embedding* (subordination), i.e. setting one plot inside the other. One can add, after Hayden White (1973), that, like a historian, a social scientist confronts 'a veritable chaos of events *already constituted*, out of which he must choose the elements of the story he would tell' (p. 6, footnote 5). Thus the necessity for two additional tactics: *exclusion* and *emphasis* (also, embedding can serve both combination and selection). Outcome-embedded stories have plots subordinated to one another in a sequence (the outcome of one episode determines the plot of the next), whereas the ending-embedded stories have all plots subordinated to the one that is revealed at the end (Mandler, 1984).

Temporal connections are not enough: a narrative whose elements are connected by *succession* only ('It rained on Monday, I bought a car on Tuesday'), is not a story. To become a plotted story, the elements, or episodes, need also to be related by *transformation* (Todorov, 1978/1990). This can be achieved by adding a third episode ('I have had enough of for ever getting wet when biking'). The episodes are still sequential but chronology now also stands for causality. An emplotted narrative thus involves not only a syntagmatic dimension but also a paradigmatic one: actions and events are not only connected but also transformed (substituted). Adding new elements is an exercise in mimesis; it does not make a narrative into a story. This is the meaning of the traditional criticism of scientific texts that are 'only descriptive'. Theory is the plot of a thesis.

Marie-Laure Ryan (1993; see Chapter 1) made a useful list of steps to be taken in the work of emplotment:

- Constructing *characters* (which, in social science texts, are often non-human: an economic decline, growing unemployment, a new computer technology).
- Attributing *functions* to single events and actions.
- Finding an *interpretative theme*.

The chronology of this list is somewhat convoluted: while an interpretative theme is found via construction of characters and attributing functions to events and actions, once found it rules over the other two. In other words, an interpretative theme emerges while the writer is trying out characters and functions but, once it has been decided upon, the text needs a tighter adjustment: thus the saying that, after having written the last chapter, one has to go back and rewrite the rest.

As I said before, there is a tendency in social science texts, not only in economics, for ending-embedded plots. All the text is supposed to be geared toward 'the conclusions'. Yet there is a possibility that the outcome of one episode will change the structure – of the next episode or of the whole text. The writer might admit to the readers that the first hypothesis had not worked and that the whole study had to change accordingly. In the next section I shall quote an example of such a complex and unexpected plot.

A story rich in plots

I shall now examine a monograph that contains several plots, uses both temporal connections (sequentiality) and causal connections (both causality and intentionality), and joins succession and transformation. It has three main characters – Aramis, the Master, and his Pupil – and its interpretative theme (a thesis of a thesis) is that when humans fail to love machines properly, the machines die. All the events and actions are subordinated to this theme.

Aramis or the Love of Technology (Latour, 1996) is a story of an automated train system that was tried in Paris and then abandoned. It begins, innocently enough, as a combination of two classic plots, one a detective story (who killed Aramis?) and the other a *Bildungsroman*, a story of a pupil learning from the master. The first plot depends for its pull on curiosity – the readers know the effects, Aramis is dead and buried in the Museum of Technology, and the cause is looked for – who did it? The second plot, embedded in the first, depends on the push of (mild) suspense: given Pupil's hunger for knowledge and Master's abundance of it, the readers might fairly surely expect an enlightened Pupil in the end, but they may count on various complications in his way.

Complications, when they arrive, are not of the manageable kind that is the stuff of fairytales. The obstacles stand in the way, not only of the heroes or their action programs but also of the plots. The main plot, that of detecting those guilty of killing an innovation, proves to be unfeasible. At a certain point there are twenty contradictory interpretations offered for the demise of the Aramis project (Latour himself counts them elsewhere), all of them correct. Just before the final report has to be produced, the Master vanishes, not because the Pupil has to learn autonomy but because the Master has more important things to think about.

What was a detective story turns into a tragic love story. Aramis has not been killed; it is just that nobody loved him enough to keep him alive. His less attractive rival, the metro system VAL, is loved and lives happily in Lille; a new Aramis is being born in San Diego – will it live?

The *Bildungsroman* turns into its opposite, a tormented inner journey of the Master into self-reflection, doubt, and fear. The Pupil gets his grade and tries to ignore the ramblings of his former Master, whose excessive reflection makes him turn against the sacred values of science. Hardly a conventional ending for a social science study.

The device of changing horses in the middle of the river (that is, transforming the main plots of the story) is a tricky business. One danger is obvious: the author might drown. Aramis, Master, and their author survive the journey very well, but it does take a masterly driver. Another danger is with the readers: they may not like the play of plots as demonstrated in Bronwyn Davies' study (1989; see Chapter 6). Readers might resort to murder in order to save 'their' plots, at least symbolically.

Latour saved himself by doing a revolutionary transformation of plots but landing with another set of recognizable and legitimate plots. His text assumes a reader well familiar with all the variety of plots in both fiction and sociology. Such tricks may well be lost on some readers, but the main trick – emplotment – is exemplary even if not easily imitated.

How can this emplotment be characterized? The text is coherent (actions and events have functions consistent with its interpretative scheme). At no point does the reader need to ask him or herself: 'Why does he tell me this?' It has a basic plot structure and then plays around it: by complicating it, by introducing subplots and counter-plots. In other words, a rich plot equals a well thought-out theory, which in social science monographs, unlike in novels, is explicitly articulated (at the end or at the beginning).

Does this mean that the conventional structure needs to be abandoned? Not necessarily. My plea is that writers understand the purpose of the conventional structure and cease to treat it mechanically. Once understood, it can be followed, abandoned, or circumvented: it may become a frame within which a well plotted story is inserted.

A simple plot that works

While Latour's text is a monograph reporting a field study, the other text I chose as an exemplar is usually classified as an essay in the history of ideas. This is Albert O. Hirschman's *The Passions and the Interests* (1977/1997). But it could be claimed that it is also a field study – a monograph in the history of economic thought. I perceive such blurring of genres as very fruitful: indeed, from the point of view of crafting the research text, there is no crucial difference between a field of practice and a field of theory, when the latter is considered a practice. An enunciation by a French engineer in

Latour's story can be analyzed in the same way as one by Montesquieu in Hirschman's.

Hirschman's book proposes a striking thesis (interpretative scheme) which it then proves: contrary to most contemporary thinking, 'interests' are not the opposite of 'passions'. Self-interest, that founding stone of capitalism, was chosen as the least wicked passion, able to curb others. His characters are basically schools of thought, represented by, but not identical to, their spokesmen (no woman among them), famous writers.

The structure of the book is simplicity itself. It contains three parts: (1) How the Interests were Called Upon to Counteract the Passions; (2) How Economic Expansion was Expected to Improve the Political Order; and (3) Reflections on Episode in Intellectual History (observe how the titles practically tell the story).

The first part is located in the Renaissance, as the epoch characterized by a new turn in the theory of the state. It had been felt that religion was no longer capable of restraining the destructive passions of human beings. Three alternatives have been considered: coercion and repression, education (socialization, indoctrination), and fighting passions with passions. Hirschman examines various circumstances that helped to establish the dominance of the last alternative in the seventeenth century. Machiavelli is an important source in this context. The attention moves to defining a passion that would have such a benevolent effect, with the well-known result that 'One set of passions, hitherto known variously as greed, avarice, or love of lucre, could be usefully employed to oppose and bridle such other passions as ambition, lust for power, or sexual lust' (Hirschman, 1977/1997: 41).

The second part explains why this thesis attracted so little attention in political sciences and economic thought of later ages. Hirschman shows that while Montesquieu in France, for example, developed the thought that economic pursuits will improve political governance, Adam Smith disconnected the two, giving an economic, no longer political, justification to the pursuit of self-interest. In his view, 'politics is the province of the "folly of men" while economic progress, like Candide's garden, can be cultivated with success provided such folly does not exceed some fairly ample and flexible limits' (1977/1997: 104).

In the third part, Hirschman briefly takes up the developments in economic and political thought that followed (he then extended his analysis to the nineteenth and twentieth centuries in his *Rival Views of Market Society*, 1992). He shows how different are the present views of market and economy from those that are claimed to be their antecedents. His reflection concerns, most of all, a phenomenon rarely focused by other scholars: *the intended but unrealized effects of ideas and decisions.*

Several aspects of Hirschman's way of emplotment can be brought to light. To begin with, although chronology is obviously an element in a historical essay, it does not have a structuring function here. The essay is structured by an outcome-bounded causality: the first part presents the first episode in political thought, which is the basis of the second episode. The second episode, however, changes the outcome and therefore the future plot. The second episode ends up in a transformation: what started as a way of solving a political problem ended by being a justification for the autonomy of economy. The third part makes this transformation obvious and ironic: 'In sum, capitalism was supposed to accomplish exactly what was soon to be denounced as its worst feature' (p. 132).

How are the two first parts composed internally, if not sequentially? As Hirschman says himself, in the first part he puts his thesis together in 'the laborious way … from bits and pieces of intellectual evidence' (p. 69). Once it has been assembled, he sets it against various later schools of thought in the second part, to look for its traces. The plot tends toward Satire.

There are several reasons for my choosing Hirschman's book as an example here. The most obvious is that Hirschman is a superb writer (an expression used by Amarthya Sen in a preface to the 1997 edition), and all his books can be recommended as models for aspiring social scientists. The second reason is that Hirschman is truly a social scientist – while practically all disciplines claim his belongingness, he himself does not see much reason to observe disciplinary borders. Thirdly, *Passions and Interests* reacquired an uncanny relevance in times when it has become painfully clear that greed does not harness violence. After coercion and indoctrination failed as well, are there any alternatives left? Are there any new ones emerging? Hirschman's text is important because of its contents and because of its form. Paying attention to the latter will only enhance the former.

While the readers of this book might not be aiming at the stylistic heights of Hirschman and Latour (although why not?), my hope is to persuade them to develop a habit of semiotic reading. After having admired a scientific text for what it says, it is useful to ask how it says it. When habitual, such reflection may pay off generously in one's own work.

Social science texts, as a family of subgenres, might thus make skillful use of narratives (although not only); it might also use the insights of literary theory as help in self-reflection. This can ease the escape from the inherited image of social science as a (still) defective natural science. I do not suggest that it should become a fiction instead. I argue for a conscious and reflective creation of a family of genres which recognizes its tradition without being paralyzed by it, which seeks inspiration in other genres without imitating them, and which derives confidence from the importance of its topic and from its own growing skills.

EXERCISE

Exercise 9.1: write your thesis!

FURTHER READING

Atkinson, Paul (1990) *The Ethnographic Imagination. Textual Construction of Reality*. London: Routledge.

Booth, Wayne C., Colomb, Gregory G., and Williams, Joseph M. (1995) *The Craft of Research*. Chicago, IL: University of Chicago Press.

Golden-Biddle, Karen, and Locke, Karen D. (1997) *Composing Qualitative Research*. Thousand Oaks, CA: Sage.

Hart, Chris (1998) *Doing a Literature Review. Releasing the Social Science Research Imagination*. London: Sage.

Van Maanen, John (1988) *Tales of the Field. On Writing Ethnography*. Chicago, IL: University of Chicago Press.

Notes

1   This chapter is partly based on my 'Writing a social science monograph', in Clive Seale, et al. (eds) *Qualitative Research Practice* (Czarniawska, 2003c).

2   There exist excellent sources that treat them separately: Becker (1986), Clifford and Marcus (1986), Hart (1998).

3   In his 'Del rigor en la ciencia' (*Historia universal de la infamia*, 1935/1967) Borges tells a story of cartographers who created a map that was identical to the empire it represented. The next generation threw away the map and forgot cartography.

4   Three volumes that are especially recommended to an interested reader are Levine (1993), R.H. Brown (1995), Van Maanen (1995).

5   This is also relevant for pictorial representations of the world.

6   I review these in *A Narrative Approach to Organization Studies* (1998).

7   I am not suggesting that the field of theory isn't politically structured, but it is usually easier to grasp its structure and choose one's strategy (joining the mainstream, joining the avant-garde, opposing the mainstream, etc.).

8   I develop this theme in *Narrating the Organization* (1997) and in *Writing Management* (1999).

10

Narrativizing Social Sciences

> The social sciences are talking sciences, and achieve in texts, not elsewhere, the observ-
> ability and practical objectivity of their phenomena. This is done in literary enterprises
> through the arts of reading and writing texts, ... and by 'shoving words around'.
> (Garfinkel et al., 1981: 133)

Garfinkel, Lynch, and Livingston should know: they have watched labora-
tory science long enough to see how it differs from the social sciences – and
how it is similar, too. But not everybody is so matter of fact in the question of
'talking sciences'. Although the attraction of narrative devices seems to be
growing among social scientists, there are plenty of qualms about their use. Let
me review some of the most common.

The dangerous stories from the field

One of the common worries, even among authors devoted to a narrative
approach, is the status of narrative material collected in the field. 'Facts, fictions,
and fantasies' runs the subtitle of Gabriel's book on organizational storytelling,
and he warns his readers, potential story collectors, of the danger

> of allowing our current fascination with text and narrative to occlude deeper issues
> of justice, politics, and human suffering ... Treating a story simply as text, disregard-
> ing the extent to which it deviates from or distorts facts and ignoring the effort and
> ingenuity that it demands, does grave injustice to story and storyteller alike. (Gabriel,
> 2000: 241)

There are several worries in this warning and I will try to unpack them one by one. The first is that fictive stories do not inform the readers of the state of the world. This criticism becomes especially relevant in the face of the fact that many promoters of a narrative approach point out that there exist a great variety of fictive narratives about various fields of practice (Waldo, 1968; Coser, 1963/1972; Czarniawska-Joerges and Guillet de Monthoux, 1994). The critique of fiction in scientific work is often grounded in a confusion of two ways of understanding fiction: as that which does not exist and that which is not true (Lamarque, 1990). If we separate these two, it becomes obvious that Kafka's Castle did not exist, and yet everything that was said about it may be true in the sense that it appears as insightful and credible in light of other texts on the absurdities of impersonal bureaucracy.

But Gabriel's (2000) worry concerns the impossibility of telling facts from fictions in stories from the field. He agrees that fictive stories are interesting and worth analyzing, but he is afraid that they will be taken for facts. Indeed, it has been pointed out that there are no structural differences between fictional and factual narratives (Veyne, 1988; see Chapter 1). How can a field researcher know which is which?

A social science researcher knows *that* facts are fabricated (Latour, 1993b; Knorr Cetina, 1994) and wishes to know *how* they are fabricated. It is therefore up to the researcher to check the production certificate (by many a well-known method, like comparing stories, checking written documents, doing source analysis, etc.) or else take part in the production – that is, making this checking process part of the research results. 'Buying tall tales' is not a requirement of a narrative approach.

Yet another possibility is that of shifting the focus from 'what does a text say?' to 'what does a text do?' ('how does a text say what it says?'), thus eliminating the question: fact or fiction? But such 'treating a story simply as a text' seems to Gabriel to do injustice to the story and to the storyteller – that is, to the social world. This danger is hard to understand, however. Looking for 'worlds in texts' is not an expression of disinterest in justice, politics, and human suffering; it is founded in the ideas shared by ethnomethodologists and post-structuralists that texts are part of the world and need to be analyzed as such. One may think that text analysis is a good way of approaching the world or not, but it must not be mistaken for indifference toward the world.

The worrisome stories of the field

But worries about the status of the narrative material are relatively small compared to the worries about a 'narrativized' social science. Does anything go in social science writing?

The first worry reflects the one formulated above, except that this time it concerns 'the stories of the field'. How does one know whether a research report is 'true' if it openly admits to a use of narrative devices, of employing metaphors and concocting stories?

> To argue ... that the writing of ethnography involves telling stories, making pictures, concocting symbolisms, and deploying tropes is commonly resisted, often fiercely, because of a confusion, endemic in the West since Plato at least, of the imagined with the imaginary, the fictional with the false, making things out with making them up. (Geertz, 1988: 140)

Traditionally, a social science text was expected to demonstrate its 'validity' (that is, its correspondence to the world) and 'reliability' (the guarantee that the same method will bring the same results). Alas, the correspondence theory of truth is untenable because the only things with which we can compare statements are other statements (Rorty, 1980). Whether one claims to speak of a reality or a fantasy, the value of utterances cannot be established by comparing them to their object but only by comparing them to other utterances. Words cannot be compared to worlds, and a look into actual validation practices reveals that they always consist in checking texts against other texts.

It could be argued that the same observation shows that there exists reliability understood as replication. From the perspective held here, however, it could be claimed that results are repeated not because the correct method has repeatedly been applied to the same object of study but because institutionalized research practices tend to produce similar results. One can go even further and claim that results are as much part of practice as methods are. It is perhaps more accurate to speak of 'conformity' rather than reliability; it is not the results that are reliable but the researchers – who are conforming to dominant rules.

Dissatisfaction with positivist criteria for 'good scientific texts' and a wish for alternative guidelines led to a search for a new set of criteria – within the interpretive tradition. Thus Guba (1981) spoke of 'trustworthiness' of naturalist studies (composed of truth value, applicability, consistency, and neutrality); Fisher (1987) spoke of 'narrative probability' (coherence) and 'narrative fidelity' (truth value), constituting 'narrative rationality'; while Golden-Biddle and Locke (1993) suggested authenticity, plausibility, and criticality as the ways in which ethnographic texts convince their audiences. Unfortunately, like the positivist criteria they criticize, these are again *ostensive* criteria of a text's success (i.e. the attributes of a text that can be demonstrated and therefore applied a priori to determine a text's success).

Reader-response theory has counteracted such objectivist reading theories (Iser, 1978) but, in turn, it subjectivized the act of reading, neglecting the institutional effect. Yet there is a limited repertoire of texts and responses at any given time and place, there are more and less legitimate responses, and there is fashion as a selection mechanism. The pragmatist theory of reading to which I am committed (Rorty, 1992) gives preference to *performative* criteria. These are not rules which, when observed by a writer, will guarantee the positive reception of his or her work, but descriptions that summarize typical justifications given when a positive reception occurs. Such descriptions do not concern the text but, rather, the responses of the readers as reported in the legitimate vocabulary of the day.

But the worries do not end. How is the reader to tell that he or she is reading social science and not fiction? It is perhaps not by accident that it is another anthropologist, Margery Wolf, who worries about 'how one is to differentiate ethnography from fiction, other than in preface, footnotes, and other authorial devices' (1992: 56). What can be said to be specific to social science writing – at least in terms of frequent use if not of intrinsic characteristics? Is there any 'core' to this genre?

As pointed out by McCloskey (1990a), social sciences use the whole tetrad of literary devices: facts and metaphors, logic and stories. While the methods of association tend toward logic without ever reaching it (one could speak of a 'logical stylization'), the methods of substitution are contained between metaphor and analogy. However, in genre analysis, the methods of substitution attract far greater attention than the methods of association. One reason could be that the eighteenth-century ideal of science landed the social sciences in a country of *things*, where nouns (names) matter most. It has been assumed that, once you get your metaphors right, the story will tell itself. If the 'sociology of verbs' as postulated by John Law (1994) ever takes hold, however, the obscure arrows standing for vague connections, as in 'it causes', 'it influences', or 'it relates to', will become the focus of social science. Causes how? Influences by what means? As Dvora Yanow (1996) provocatively asked, 'How does a policy mean?' Reflection upon the modes of association has yet to be developed in the texts of the social sciences.

Thus, the danger of social science being taken for literary fiction seems rather distant (the known cases were the other way around, that is, works suspected of being a fiction presenting themselves as social science, like it was the case with Castaneda[1]). Consequently, the worry that by engaging in literary work, social scientists will become literary critics, thus problematizing the legitimacy of their own endeavor and/or losing out in competition with literary theorists, is not very substantial. This concern is a historical echo of a similar concern voiced when social sciences quite unreflectively imitated natural sciences, an imitation that, like every process of translation, brought about some very interesting and some less interesting results. No scientific discipline is, or has ever been, autarchic, so the question is not whether to imitate but whom and how. It is therefore time to consider the promises and hopes that a narrative approach, and the rapprochement with literature and literary theory it implies, might bring to social sciences.

The hopeful narratives

To me, a narrative approach to social sciences opens at least three opportunities. The first is the extended use of texts as field material, connected to a variety of techniques permitting a text analysis. Factual or fictional, texts are the daily bread of social scientists, and the traditional preference for fabricating texts rather than collecting them might have been partly caused by an uncertainty about what to do with them. The typical solution to this problem was to count the texts (or anything in them that could be counted), and afterwards proceed as usual in social sciences (content analysis is, after all, an early example of the use of structuralism in social sciences). While quantification of texts and texts' elements might make perfect sense in many a context, it does not solve the problem of interpretation. A 'counted text' is a new text that must be interpreted.

Here the question 'how to imitate' reappears. I signaled my stance while ironizing the ideas of 'proper deconstruction' and 'correctly applied structural analysis'. Here is actually the ground for a differentiation between a theory of literature and a theory of society. While students of literature must show themselves worthy apprentices of such craftsmen as Derrida and Barthes, students of society must be able to say something interesting about society. In order to accomplish that, they need to move like all other readers, who, in de Certeau's metaphor, 'move across lands belonging to someone else, like nomads poaching their way across the fields they did not write, despoiling the wealth of Egypt to enjoy it themselves' (1984/1988: 174). Poaching the other field's methods and techniques but setting them to their own use. I do not think that there exists anything that must, should, or ought to 'be done' to narratives. Every reading is an interpretation, and every interpretation is an association: tying the text that is interpreted to other texts, other voices, other times and places. Much more important than a specific interpretative or analytical technique is the result: an interesting recontextualization.

The second opportunity is creative borrowing of writing itself. 'Hybridizing the genre' would perhaps be a fitting expression:

> To the few wooden tongues developed in academic journals, we should add the many genres and styles of narration invented by novelists, journalists, artists, cartoonists, scientists and philosophers. The reflexive character of our domain will be recognized in the future by the multiplicity of genres, not by the tedious presence of 'reflexive loops'. (Latour, 1988: 173)

What Margery Wolf said of anthropology could be applied to all social sciences. Each of them 'is a discipline with very permeable borders, picking up methodologies, theories, and data from any source whatever that can provide the answers to our questions' (Wolf, 1992: 51). All these 'loans' arrive in packages typical of the genre from which they have come. Traditionally, however, social scientists tended to ignore 'the form', insisting that it is the 'pure contents' that are being tapped. Latour's advice amounts to suggesting making a virtue out of a vice, an art out of an unreflective behavior.

The third opportunity is therefore genre reflection and analysis. The debate on what is good and bad writing can be replaced or at least aided by a discussion of genres (i.e. institutionalized forms of writing). A genre analysis will reveal how institutional classifications are made and will thus render the works of science more comprehensible.

But genre analysis is also a genre construction, an institution building, and as such it invites policing attempts: somebody must 'protect the core'. As genre analysis in literature has shown, however, such protective policing leads to the suffocation of a genre in the worst case, to nothing in many cases, and to a development of a genre in the best case, as happened to the detective story (Czarniawska, 1999a). Neither paradoxicality nor conflict weakens a genre; on the contrary, they enhance its controlling power. And among the authors who operate in the gray zones are innovators: those who rejuvenate and reform the genre.

Achieving an inventory and a description of genres not only allows for probabilistic estimates of success but also allows us to understand deviations. Every avant-garde, every vibrant fringe, every edifying discourse feeds on the mainstream, on normal science, on systematizing discourse. By the same token, the 'canonical tradition' (MacIntyre, 1988) depends on deviations for its survival, and also owes its eventual demise to them.

In my rendition, the narrative approach to social sciences does not offer a 'method'; neither does it have a 'paradigm', a set of procedures to check the correctness of its results. It gives access to an ample bag of tricks – from traditional criticism through formalists to deconstruction – but it steers away from the idea that a 'rigorously' applied procedure would render 'testable' results. The use of narrative devices in social sciences should lead to more inspired reading, as Rorty (1992) calls it, and an inspired – and inspiring – writing.

This book, as should be obvious by now, is grounded in a belief that social science, in order to matter more in the life of contemporary societies,[2] needs to reach readers outside its own circles. While the texts of disciplinary self-reflection will remain interesting and relevant for social scientists only (which does not mean that they should abandon any literary pretensions – social scientists love beautiful texts, too), the bulk of social science needs to be skillfully crafted. And the questions – from inside and outside – such as: 'is it valid?' 'is it reliable?' 'is it Science?' should be replaced by such questions as: is it interesting? Is it relevant? Is it beautiful? In other words, I suggest that social scientists enter into a double contract with their readers, fictional *and* referential: suspend disbelief, as I intend to please you, but also activate disbelief, as I intend to instruct you. I have no doubts that the readers will manage both: after all, they are doing it all the time.

FURTHER READING

Boje, David (2001) *Narrative Methods for Organizational and Communication Research.* London: Sage.
Brown, Richard Harvey (1998) *Toward a Democratic Science. Scientific Narration and Civic Communication.* New Haven, CT: Yale University Press.
Czarniawska, Barbara and Gagliardi, Pasquale (eds) (2003) *Narratives We Organize by.* Amsterdam: John Benjamins.
Flyvbjerg, Bent (2001) *Making Social Science Matter: Why Social Inquiry Fails and How It Can Succeed Again.* Cambridge: Cambridge University Press.
Gabriel, Yiannis (ed.) (2004) *Myths, Stories, and Organizations: Premodern Narratives of Our Times.* Oxford: Oxford University Press.

Notes

1 Carlos Castaneda's *The Teachings of Don Juan* (1968) is a dissertation on the sociology of knowledge where Don Juan, the 'native informant', introduces Castaneda to a system of knowledge alternative to the Western one (and mediated by hallucinogenic drugs).
2 See also Flyvbjerg's impassionate call for 'a social science that matters' (2001).

Glossary

Actant
A central notion in Algirdas Greimas' version of structural analysis. Actant is 'that which accomplishes or undergoes an act' (Greimas and Courtés, 1982: 5). It has been introduced to replace the terms 'character' and *dramatis persona* as it applies not only to human beings but also to animals, objects, and concepts.

Apology (*also* apologia)
A speech or a text presenting a defense or a justification (of somebody or something) against an actual or potential accusation. For example, it is sometimes claimed that social sciences are *apologetic* about the use of power. It is different from **eulogy** in that it admits the potentiality of a critique.

Bildungsroman
A novel describing the protagonist's formative years, spiritual education, or a quest for knowledge. It is about education but its intention is to educate the reader.

Dramatist analysis
An analytic scheme proposed by Kenneth Burke (1945/1969) that checks the congruence between five aspects of a story: Scene, Act, Agent, Agency, and Purpose (the so-called Burke's Pentad).

Emplotment (*also* plotting)
A term coined by Hegel in his 'theory of historical emplotment', popularized by Hayden White (1973). Originally used in the context of historical works, it meant an introduction of a literary structure into a chronological account, thus turning it into a 'history'.

Ending-embedded plot
A story in which the logical connection between various episodes becomes visible in the end; the end justifies the structure of the story (*see also* **outcome-embedded plot**).

Eulogy (*also* eulogia)
A speech or a text filled with praise and commendation for a person or a thing; opposite of critique (*see also* **apology**).

Exegesis
A thorough exposition complete with glosses and explanations. Originally, the critical interpretation of a biblical text to discover its intended meaning.

Formalism
The term comes from mathematics and denotes a view that mathematics concerns manipulation of symbols according to prescribed structural rules. Applied to arts,

it is a view that in interactions with works of art, form should be given primacy. This view was espoused by a Russian group of literary theorists in the 1920s.

Hermeneutic circle (*also* hermeneutic spiral, hermeneutic arc)
The assumption, in the theory of interpretation, that the unknown can only be comprehended via the mediation of what is already known.

Hermeneutics
Originally denoting the theory of interpretation of the Scriptures, it is now used more generally to signify the philosophy and theory of interpretation.

Hyperbole
A rhetorical device consisting in using exaggerated or extravagant terms – for emphasis.

Hypothyposis
A visually powerful, vivid description.

Intentio auctoris
A theory of interpretation that assumes that the purpose of reading is to deduce the author's intentions (originally, God's intentions in the Scriptures).

Intentio lectoris
A theory of interpretation that suggests looking for the reader's intentions (that is, the reader's reception of a text).

Intentio operis
A term coined by Umberto Eco (1992) in opposition to an idea of a 'unlimited semiosis' – that is, the idea that each text can be interpreted in unlimited numbers of ways. While the text says both more and less than its author intended, its readers rarely interpret it whimsically or randomly.

Kairos
The Greek god of 'right' or 'proper' time, different from *Chronos*, who took care of 'linear' time. *Kairotic* time is punctuated by important events, not by time units; it does not 'pass' but 'runs forward' or 'stands still'.

Metonymy
A rhetorical trope that substitutes cause for effect or effect for cause (where causality is sometimes deduced from proximity in space or time), or a proper name for one of its qualities or vice versa.

Mimesis
Imitation; of another person's words or actions but also representation of the world in poetry, prose, and art.

Narrative trajectory
One of the concepts in Algirdas Greimas' version of structuralist analysis: a logically connected chain of narrative programs (changes of state produced by actants).

Outcome-embedded plot
A story in which the contents of an episode are the consequence of the outcome of the previous episode; the structure of the story is contingent on what happens in the story (*see also* **end-embedded plot**).

Paradigm
In the context of narrative, the way in which the elements in a narrative can be replaced by one another; the mode of substitution (*see also* **syntagm**).

Polyphony
Many voices speaking in a text (as opposed to monophony, where only the narrator has a voice). Close to it is Bakhtin's (1928/1985) concept of variegated speech (*heteroglossia*) where there are not only many voices but where they also speak in different dialects.

Poststructuralism
A reaction to, but also a continuation of, **structuralism**. A deconstructive approach to texts, revealing their structure as imposed or constructed, often in spite of the author's declared intentions.

Reader-response theory
The theory of interpretation according to which meaning is the product of an interaction between a text and a reader (Iser, 1978). Thus, the text or the author does not determine the text's interpretation, but neither are readers free to interpret as they wish. The term is close to Eco's ***intentio operis***, but gives equal importance to the text and the reader.

Semantics
A theory of meaning; different from semiology/semiotics.

Semiology; semiotics
A theory of signs. The first term is often used in the continental context (the term was introduced by the Swiss linguist, Ferdinand de Saussure), the second in the Anglo-Saxon context (the term was introduced by John Locke and elaborated by Charles Peirce).

Signature
The visible presence of the author's voice in a text, or lack of it. Geertz (1988) speaks of 'author-saturated' (visible signature) and 'author-evacuated' (effaced signature) texts.

Structuralism
A distinctive but varied school of thought in the social and human sciences. It is possible to speak about US structuralism (initiated by the linguist, Leonard Bloomfield, and popularized by Noam Chomsky) and European structuralism (beginning with the Swiss linguist, Ferdinand de Saussure, and continuing with Claude Lévi-Strauss, Algirdas Greimas, et al.). It looks for 'deep structures' in discourses and texts that are supposed to express 'human nature', 'the basic structure of the language', or 'the character of a society'.

Synecdoche
A rhetorical trope that substitutes part for whole, genus for species, or vice versa.

Syntagm (*also* syntagma)
The way the elements in a narrative are connected to each other; the mode of association (*see also* **paradigm**).

Travelogue
A text, film, or illustrated lecture about places and people encountered in the course of travel.

Notes

Apart from works quoted directly, this glossary has been compiled with the help of the following sources:

Audi, Robert (ed.) (1995) *The Cambridge Dictionary of Philosophy*. Cambridge: Cambridge University Press.

Encyclopaedia Britannica (1989) Chicago, IL: Encyclopaedia Britannica.

Greimas, Algirdas Julien and Courtés, Joseph (1982) *Semiotics and Language. An Analytical Dictionary*. Bloomington, IN: Indiana University Press.

Lanham, Richard A. (1991) *A Handlist of Rhetorical Terms*. Berkeley, CA: University of California Press.

Oxford English Dictionary, The New Shorter (1993) Oxford: Clarendon Press.

Sini, Carlo (ed.) (1992) *Filosofia (Dizionario)*. Milan: Jaca Book.

References

Agger, Ben (1990) *The Decline of Discourse. Reading, Writing and Resistance in Postmodern Capitalism*. Bristol, PA: Falmer Press.

Akins, Kathleen (1993) 'What is it like to be boring and myopic?', in Bo Dahlbom (ed.) *Dennet and His Critics*. Oxford: Blackwell, 124–60.

Apolito, Paolo (1990) *Dice che hanno visto la Madonna*. Bologna: Il Mulino. English translation (1998): *Apparitions of the Madonna at Oliveto Citra*. University Park, PA: Pennsylvania State University Press.

Ashmore, Malcolm (1989) *The Reflexive Thesis. Wrighting Sociology of Scientific Knowledge*. Chicago, IL: University of Chicago Press.

Atkinson, Paul (1990) *The Ethnographic Imagination. Textual Constructions of Reality*. London: Routledge.

Atkinson, Paul, and Silverman, David (1997) 'Kundera's *Immortality*: the interview society and the invention of the self,' *Qualitative Inquiry*, 3 (3): 304–25.

Audi, Robert (ed.) (1995) *The Cambridge Dictionary of Philosophy*. Cambridge: Cambridge University Press.

Bakhtin, Mikhail M. (1981) 'Discourse in the novel', in Mikhail Bakhtin, *The Dialogic Imagination. Four Essays*. Austin, TX: University of Texas Press, 259–422.

Bakhtin, Mikhail M./Medvedev, P.N. (1928/1985) *The Formal Method in Literary Scholarship. A Crtitical Introduction to Sociological Poetics*. Cambridge, MA: Harvard University Press.

Barthes, Roland (1966/1977) 'Introduction to the structural analysis of narratives', in Roland Barthes, *Image-Music-Text* (trans. Stephen Heath). Glasgow: Collins, 79–124.

Barthes, Roland (1979) 'From work to text', in Josué V. Harrari (ed.) *Textual Strategies. Perspectives in Post-structuralist Criticism*. Ithaca, NY: Methuen, 73–81.

Bartlett, Frederick C. (1932) *Remembering: A Study in Experimental and Social Psychology*. Cambridge: Cambridge University Press.

Becker, Howard (1986) *Writing for Social Scientists*. Chicago, IL: University of Chicago Press.

Berger, Peter, and Luckmann, Thomas (1966) *The Social Construction of Reality*. New York, NY: Doubleday.

Berman, Marshall (1992) 'Why modernity still matters', in Scott Lash and Jonathan Friedman (eds) *Modernity and Identity*. Oxford: Blackwell, 33–58.

Bittner, Egon (1965) 'The concept of organization', *Social Research*, 31: 240–55.

Boje, David (1991) 'The story-telling organization: a study of story performance in an office-supply firm', *Administrative Science Quarterly*, 36: 106–26.

Boje, David (2001) *Narrative Methods for Organizational and Communication Research*. London: Sage.

Boland, Richard J. Jr, and Tenkasi, Ramkrishnan V. (1995) 'Perspective making and perspective taking in communities of knowing', *Organization Science*, 6 (3): 350–72.

Booth, Wayne C., Colomb, Gregory G., and Williams, Joseph M. (1995) *The Craft of Research*. Chicago, IL: University of Chicago Press.

Bourdieu, Pierre (1990) *The Logic of Practice*. Oxford: Polity Press.

Brown, Richard H. (1977) *A Poetic for Sociology: Toward a Logic of Discovery for the Human Sciences*. New York, NY: Cambridge University Press.

Brown, Richard H. (1987) *Society as Text. Essays on Rhetoric, Reason and Reality*. Chicago, IL: University of Chicago Press.

Brown, Richard H. (1989) *Social Science as Civic Discourse. Essays on the Invention, Legitimation, and Uses of Social Theory*. Chicago, IL: The University of Chicago Press.

Brown, Richard H. (ed.) (1995) *Postmodern Representations: Truth, Power and Mimesis in the Human Sciences and Public Culture*. Chicago, IL: University of Illinois Press.

Brown, Richard H. (1998) *Toward a Democratic Science: Scientific Narration and Civic Communication*. New Haven, CT: Yale University Press.

Bruner, Jerome (1986) *Actual Minds, Possible Worlds*. Cambridge, MA: Harvard University Press.

Bruner, Jerome (1990) *Acts of Meaning*. Cambridge, MA: Harvard University Press.

Bruss, Elisabeth W. (1976) *Autobiographical Acts. The Changing Situation of the Literary Genre*. Baltimore, MD: Johns Hopkins University Press.

Burke, Kenneth (1945/1969) *A Grammar of Motives*. Berkeley, CA: University of California Press.

Burke, Kenneth (1968) 'Dramatism', in *International Encyclopaedia of the Social Sciences*, *VII*. New York, NY: Macmillan, 445–52.

Burrell, Gibson (1984) 'Sex and organizational analysis'. *Organization Studies*, 5 (2): 97–118.

Calás, Marta B., and Smircich, Linda (1991) 'Voicing seduction to silence leadership', *Organization Studies*, 12 (4): 567–601.

Cappetti, Carla (1993) *Writing Chicago. Modernism, Ethnography and the Novel*. New York, NY: Columbia University Press.

Castaneda, Carlos (1968/1986) *The Teachings of Don Juan*. Harmordsworth: Penguin.

Clark, Burton R. (1972) 'The organizational saga in higher education', *Administrative Science Quarterly*, 17: 178–84.

Clifford, James, and Marcus, George E. (eds) (1986), *Writing Culture. The Poetics and Politics of Ethnography*. Berkeley, CA: University of California Press.

Connerton, Paul (1989) *How Societies Remember*. Cambridge: Cambridge University Press.

Cooren, François (2000) *The Organizing Property of Communication*. Amsterdam: John Benjamins.

Cooren, François (2001) 'Acting and organizing: how speech acts structure organizational interactions', *Concepts and Transformation*, 6 (3): 275–93.

Corvellec, Hervé (1997) *Stories of Achievement. Narrative Features of Organizational Performance*. New Brunswick, NJ: Transaction Publishers.

Coser, Lewis A. (ed.) (1963/1972) *Sociology Through Literature*. Englewood Cliffs, NJ: Prentice Hall.

Culler, Jonathan (1977) 'Foreword', in Tzvetan Todorov, *The Poetics of Prose*. Ithaca, NY: Cornell University Press, 7–13.

Curtis, Ron (1994) 'Narrative form and normative force: Baconian story-telling in popular science', *Social Studies of Science*, 24: 419–61.

Czarniawska, Barbara (1988) *Ideological Control in Nonideological Organizations*. New York: Praeger.

Czarniawska, Barbara (1997) *Narrating the Organization. Dramas of Institutional Identity.* Chicago, IL: University of Chicago Press.

Czarniawska, Barbara (1998) *A Narrative Approach in Organization Studies.* Thousand Oaks, CA: Sage.

Czarniawska, Barbara (1999a) *Writing Management. Organization Theory as a Genre.* Oxford: Oxford University Press.

Czarniawska, Barbara (1999b) 'Is it possible to be a constructionist consultant?', *Management Learning*, 32 (2): 253–72.

Czarniawska, Barbara (2000) *A City Reframed. Managing Warsaw in the 1990s.* Reading: Harwood Academic.

Czarniawska, Barbara (2002) *A Tale of Three Cities, or the Glocalization of City Management.* Oxford: Oxford University Press.

Czarniawska, Barbara (2003a) 'Social constructionism in organization studies', in Stewart Clegg, and Robert Westwood, (eds) *Debating Organizations. Point-counterpoint in Organization Studies.* Oxford: Blackwell, 128–34.

Czarniawska, Barbara (2003b) 'The uses of narrative in social science research', in Melissa Hardy and Alan Bryman (eds) *Handbook of Data Analysis.* London: Sage, 649–55.

Czarniawska, Barbara (2003c) 'Writing a social science monograph', in Clive Seale, Giampietro Gobo, Jaber F. Gubrium and David Silverman (eds) *Qualitative Research Practice.* London: Sage.

Czarniawska, Barbara, and Gagliardi, Pasquale (eds) (2003) *Narratives We Organize by.* Amsterdam: John Benjamins.

Czarniawska-Joerges, Barbara (1988) *Ideological Control in Nonideological Organizations.* New York, NY: Praeger.

Czarniawska-Joerges, Barbara (1994) 'Gender, power, organizations', in John Hassard and Martin Parker, (eds) *The New Organization Theory Revisited.* London: Routledge, 227–47.

Czarniawska-Joerges, Barbara, and Guillet de Monthoux, Pierre (eds) (1994) *Good Novels, Better Management. Reading Organizational Realities in Fiction.* Reading: Harwood Academic Press.

Czarniawska-Joerges, Barbara, and Kranas, Grazyna (1991) 'Power in the eyes of the innocent (students talk on power in organization)', *Scandinavian Journal of Management*, 7 (1): 41–60.

Davies, Bronwyn (1989) *Frogs and Snails and Feminist Tales.* North Sydney: Allen & Unwin.

Davies, Bronwyn, and Harré, Rom (1991) 'Positioning: The discursive production of selves', *Journal for the Theory of Social Behaviour*, 20 (1): 43–63.

Davis, Mike (1990) *City of Quartz: Excavating the Future in Los Angeles.* London: Vintage.

de Certeau, Michel (1984/1988) *The Practice of Everyday Life.* Berkeley, CA: University of California Press.

Denzin, Norman K., and Lincoln, Yvonne S. (2000) 'Introduction: the discipline and practice of qualitative research', in Norman K. Denzin and Yvonne S. Lincoln (eds) *Handbook of Qualitative Research* (2nd edn). Thousand Oaks, CA: Sage.

Derrida, Jacques (1976) *Of Grammatology.* Baltimore, MD: Johns Hopkins University Press.

Derrida, Jacques (1987) *The Postcard. From Socrates to Freud and Beyond.* Chicago, IL: University of Chicago Press.

de Saussure, Ferdinand (1933/1983) *Course in General Linguistic*. London: Duckworth.

DeVault, Marjorie L. (1990) 'Novel readings: the social organization of interpretation', *American Journal of Sociology*, 95 (4): 887–921.

Eco, Umberto (1989) *Foucault's Pendulum*. Orlando, FL: Harcourt Brace Jovanovich.

Eco, Umberto (1990) *The Limits of Interpretation*. Bloomington, IN: Indiana University Press.

Eco, Umberto (1992) *Interpretation and Overinterpretation*. Cambridge: Cambridge University Press.

Eco, Umberto (2003) *Mouse or Rat? Traduttore Trattative*. London: Weidenfeld & Nicholson.

Edmondson, Ricca (1984) *Rhetoric in Sociology*. London: Macmillan.

Encyclopaedia Britannica Online (accessed 14 October 2000).

Encyclopaedia Britannica (1989) Chicago, IL: Encyclopaedia Britannica.

Edwards, J.A., and Lampert, Michelle D. (eds) (1993) *Talking Data: Transcription and Coding in Discourse Research*. Hillsdale, NJ: Lawrence Erlbaum Associates.

Eräsaari, Leena (2002) 'The Black Engel – women from the ruins of the National Board of Building', in Barbara Czarniawska and Heather Höpfl (eds) *Casting the Other*. London: Routledge, 138–59.

Feldman, Martha (1995) *Strategies for Interpreting Qualitative Data*. Newbury Park, CA: Sage.

Fineman, Stephen (ed.) (1993) *Emotions in Organizations*. London: Sage.

Fish, Stanley (1989) *Doing What Comes Naturally: Change, Rhetoric, and the Practice of Theory in Literary and Legal Studies*. Durham, NC: Duke University Press.

Fisher, Walter R. (1984) 'Narration as a human communication paradigm: the case of public moral argument', *Communication Monographs*, 51: 1–22.

Fisher, Walter R. (1987) *Human Communication as Narration: Toward a Philosophy of Reason, Value, and Action*. Columbia, SC: University of South Carolina Press.

Flanagan, John C. (1954) 'The critical incident technique', *Psychological Bulletin*, 51 (4): 327–58.

Flyvbjerg, Bent (2001) *Making Social Science Matter: Why Social Inquiry Fails and How It Can Succeed again*. Cambridge: Cambridge University Press.

Foucault, Michel (1979) 'What is an author?', in Josué V. Harrari (ed.) *Textual Strategies. Perspectives in Post-structuralist Criticism*. Ithaca, NY: Methuen, 141–60.

Fournier, Valérie (2002) 'Keeping the veil of otherness: practising disconnection', in Barbara Czarniawska and Heather, Höpfl (eds) *Casting the Other: The Production and Maintenance of Inequalities in Work Organizations*. London: Routledge, 68–88.

Frye, Northrop (1957/1990) *The Anatomy of Criticism*. London: Penguin Books.

Fukuyama, Francis (1992) *The End of the History and the Last Man*. London: Hamish Hamilton.

Gabriel, Yiannis (2000) *Storytelling in Organizations*. Oxford: Oxford University Press.

Gabriel, Yiannis (ed.) (2004) *Myths, Stories, and Organizations: Premodern Narratives for Our Times*. Oxford: Oxford University Press.

Gadamer, Hans-George (1960/1975) *Truth and Method*. New York, NY: Continuum.

Garfinkel, Harold (1967) *Studies in Ethnomethodology*. Englewood Cliffs, NJ: Prentice Hall.

Garfinkel, Harold, Lynch, Michael, and Livingston, Eric (1981) 'The work of the discovering science construed with materials from the optically discovered pulsar', *Philosophy of the Social Sciences*, 11: 131–58.

Geertz, Clifford (1980) *Negara: The Theatre State in Nineteenth-century Bali*. Princeton, NJ: Princeton University Press.

Geertz, Clifford (1988) *Works and Lives: The Anthropologist as Author*. Stanford, CA: Stanford University Press.

Gherardi, Silvia (1995) *Gender, Symbolism and Organizational Culture*. London: Sage.

Glaser, Barney, and Strauss, Anselm (1967) *The Discovery of Grounded Theory*. Chicago, IL: Aldine.

Golden-Biddle, Karen, and Locke, Karen D. (1993) 'Appealing work: an investigation of how ethnographic texts convince', *Organization Science*, 4 (4): 595–616.

Golden-Biddle, Karen, and Locke, Karen D. (1997) *Composing Qualitative Research*. Thousand Oaks, CA: Sage.

Goody, Jack (1986) *The Logic of Writing and the Organization of Society*. Cambridge: Cambridge University Press.

Goody, Jack, and Watt, Ian (1968) 'The consequences of literacy', in Jack Goody (ed.) *Literacy in Traditional Societies*. Cambridge: Cambridge University Press, 27–68.

Graff, Agnieszka (2001) *Swiat bez kobiet. Plec w polskim zyciu publicznym (The World Without Women. Gender in Public Life in Poland)*. Warszawa: Wydawnictwo AB.

Greimas, Algirdas Julien and Courtés, Joseph (1982) *Semiotics and Language. An Analytical Dictionary*. Bloomington, IN: Indiana University Press.

Guba, Edwin G. (1981) 'Criteria for assessing trustworthiness of naturalistic inquiries', *Educational Communication and Technology Journal*, 29 (2): 75–91.

Gubrium, Jaber F. and Holstein, James A. (1997) *The New Language of Qualitative Research*. New York, NY: Oxford University Press.

Gubrium, Jaber F., and Holstein, James A. (2002) 'From the individual interview to the interview society', in Jaber F. Gubrium, and James A. Holstein, (eds) *Handbook of Interview Research. Context and Method*. Thousand Oaks, CA: Sage, 3–32.

Gumbrecht, Hans Ulrich (1992) *Making Sense in Life and Literature*. Minneapolis, MN: University of Minnesota Press.

Gusfield, Joseph (1976) 'The literary rhetoric of science: comedy and pathos in drinking driver research', *American Sociological Review*, 41: 16–34.

Gustavsen, Bjørn (1985) 'Workplace reform and democratic dialogue', *Economic and Industrial Democracy*, 6 (4): 461–79.

Habermas, Jürgen (1972) *Knowledge and Human Interests*. London: Heinemann.

Habermas, Jürgen (1984) *The Theory of Communicative Action*. Boston, MA: Beacon Press.

Hammersley, Martyn, and Atkinson, Paul (1995) *Ethnography. Principles in Practice* (2nd edn). London: Routledge.

Harari, Jose V. (1979) 'Critical factions/critical fictions', in Jose V. Harari, (ed.) *Textual Strategies: Perspectives in Post-structuralist Criticism*. Ithaca, NY: Methuen, 17–72.

Haraway, Donna (1991) 'A cyborg manifesto: science, technology, and socialist-feminism in the late twentieth century', in Donna Haraway, *Simians, Cyborgs and Women: The Reinvention of Nature*. New York, NY: Routledge, 149–81.

Haraway, Donna (1992) 'The promises of monsters: a regenerative politics for inappropriate/d others', in Lawrence Grosberg et al. (eds) *Cultural Studies*. London: Routledge, 295–337.

Haraway, Donna (1997) *Modest Witness @ Second Millennium FemaleMan Meets Onco Mouse*. London: Routledge.

Harré, Rom (1982) 'Theoretical preliminaries to the study of action', in Mario von Cranach and Rom Harré (eds) *The Analysis of Action*. Cambridge: Cambridge University Press, 5–33.

Hart, Chris (1998) *Doing a Literature Review. Revealing the Social Science Research Imagination*. London: Sage.

Hayles, Catherine (1993) 'Constrained constructivism: locating scientific inquiry in the theater of representation', in George Levine (ed.) *Realism and Representation: Essays on the Problem of Realism in Relation to Science, Literature and Culture*. Madison, WI: University of Wisconsin Press, 27–43.

Helmers, Sabine, and Buhr, Regina (1994) 'Corporate story-telling: the buxomly secretary, a pyrrhic victory of the male mind', *Scandinavian Journal of Management*, 10 (2): 175–92.

Herman, Ellen (1995) *The Romance of American Psychology. Political Culture in the Age of Experts*. Berkeley, CA: California University Press.

Hernadi, Paul (1987) 'Literary interpretation and the rhetoric of the human sciences', in John S. Nelson et al. (eds) *The Rhetoric of the Human Sciences*. Madison, WI: University of Wisconsin Press, 263–75.

Hirschman, Albert O. (1977/1997) *The Passions and the Interests. Political Arguments for Capitalism Before Its Triumph*. Princeton, NJ: Princeton University Press.

Hirschman, Albert O. (1992) *Rival Views of Market Society and Other Recent Essays*. Cambridge, MA: Harvard University Press.

Holstein, James A. and Gubrium, Jaber F. (1997) 'Active interviewing', in David Silverman (ed.) *Qualitative Research. Theory, Method and Practice*, London: Sage, 113–29.

Iser, Wolfgang (1978) *The Act of Reading: A Theory of Aesthetic Response*. Baltimore, MD: Johns Hopkins University Press.

Jakobson, Roman (1978) *Six Lectures on Sound and Meaning*. Hassocks: Harvester Press.

Jameson, Fredric (1981) *The Political Unconscious: Narrative as a Socially Symbolic Act*. Ithaca, NY: Cornell University Press.

Johnson, Barbara (1980) *The Critical Difference: Essays in the Contemporary Rhetoric of Reading*. Baltimore, MD: Johns Hopkins University Press.

Johnson, Jeffrey C., and Weller, Susan C. (2002) 'Elicitation techniques for interviewing', in Jaber F. Gubrium and James A. Holstein (eds) *Handbook of Interview Research. Context and Method*. Thousand Oaks, CA: Sage, 491–514.

Kartvedt, Sindre (1994/95) 'Cyberpunk sage', *Scanorama*, December/January: 54–8.

Kendall, Gavin, and Wickham, Gary (1998) *Using Foucault's Methods*. London: Sage.

Kilduff, Martin (1993) 'Deconstructing organizations', *American Management Review*, 18 (1): 13–31.

Klamer, Arjo, McCloskey, Deirdre N., and Solow, Robert M. (eds) (1988) *The Consequences of Economic Rhetoric*. Cambridge: Cambridge University Press.

Knorr Cetina, Karin (1994) 'Primitive classifications and postmodernity: towards a sociological notion of fiction', *Theory, Culture and Society*, 11: 1–22.

Kostera, Monika (1997) 'Personal performatives: collecting poetical definitions of management', *Organization*, 4 (3): 345–53.

Kostera, Monika (2002) 'Control: accounting for the lost innocence', in: Mihaela Kelemen and Monika Kostera (eds) *Managing the Transition: Critical Management Research in Eastern Europe*. Basingstoke: Palgrave, 111–27.

Kunda, Gideon (1992) *Engineering Culture: Control and Commitment in a High-tech Organization*. Philadelphia, PA: Temple University Press.

Kundera, Milan (1988) *The Art of the Novel*. London: Faber & Faber.

Kvale, Steinar (1996) *InterViews. An Introduction to Qualitative Research Interviewing.* Thousand Oaks, CA: Sage.

Labov, William, and Waletzky, Joshua (1967) 'Narrative analysis: oral versions of personal experience', in June Helms (ed.) *Essays on the Verbal and Visual Arts.* Seattle, WA: University of Washington Press, 12–44.

Lamarque, Peter (1990) 'Narrative and invention: the limits of fictionality', in Christopher Nash (ed.) *Narrative in Culture.* London: Routledge, 5–22.

Landau, Misia (1984) 'Human evolution as narrative', *American Scientist*, 72: 262–8.

Landau, Misia (1987) 'Paradise lost: terrestriality in human evolution', in John Nelson et al. (eds) *The Rhetoric of Humans Sciences.* Madison WI: University of Wisconsin Press, 111–23.

Landau, Misia (1991) *Narratives of Human Evolution.* New Haven, CT: Yale University Press.

Lanham, Richard A. (1991) *A Handlist of Rhetorical Terms.* Berkeley, CA: University of California Press.

Latour, Bruno (1988) 'An relativistic account of Einstein's relativity', *Social Studies of Science*, 18: 3–44.

Latour, Bruno (1992) 'Technology is society made durable', in John Law (ed.) *A Sociology of Monsters: Essays on Power, Technology and Domination.* London: Routledge, 103–31.

Latour, Bruno (1993a) 'Pasteur on lactic acid yeast: a partial semiotic analysis', *Configurations*, 1 (1): 129–46.

Latour, Bruno (1993b) *We Have Never Been Modern.* Cambridge, MA: Harvard University Press.

Latour, Bruno (1996) *Aramis or the Love of Technology.* Cambridge, MA: Harvard University Press.

Latour, Bruno (1999) *Pandora's Hope.* Cambridge, MA: Harvard University Press.

Latour, Bruno (2000) 'When things strike back: a possible contribution of "science studies" to the social sciences', *British Journal of Sociology*, 51 (1): 107–23.

Law, John (1994) *Organizing Modernity.* Oxford: Blackwell.

Lejeune, Philippe (1989) *On Autobiography.* Minneapolis, MN: University of Minnesota Press.

Lenoir, Timothy (1994) 'Was the last turn the right turn? The semiotic turn and A.J. Greimas', *Configurations*, 1: 119–36.

Levine, George (ed.) (1993) *Realism and Representation: Essays on the Problem of Realism in Relation to Science, Literature and Culture.* Madison, WI: University of Wisconsin Press.

Lévi-Strauss, Claude (1968) *Structural Anthropology.* London: Allen Lane.

Linde, Charlotte (1993) *Life Stories. The Creation of Coherence.* New York, NY: Oxford University Press.

Luckmann, Benita (1978) 'The small life-worlds of modern man', in Thomas Luckmann (ed.) *Phenomenology and Sociology.* Harmondsworth: Penguin Books, 275–90.

Lyotard, Jean-François (1979/1986) *The Postmodern Condition. A Report on Knowledge.* Manchester: Manchester University Press.

MacIntyre, Alasdair (1981/1990) *After Virtue.* London: Duckworth.

MacIntyre, Alasdair (1988) *Whose Justice? Which Rationality?.* London: Duckworth.

Mandler, Jean Matter (1984) *Stories, Scripts, and Scenes: Aspects of Schema Theory.* Hillsdale, NJ: Lawrence Erlbaum Associates.

Mangham, Ian L., and Overington, Michael A. (1987) *Organizations as Theatre: A Social Psychology of Dramatic Appearances.* Chichester: Wiley.

Marcus, George E. (1992) 'Past, present and emergent identities: requirements for ethnographies of late twentieth-century modernity world-wide', in Scott Lash and Jonathan Friedman (eds) *Modernity and Identity.* Oxford: Blackwell, 309–30.

Marcus, George E., and Fischer, Michael M.J. (1986) *Anthropology as Cultural Critique.* Chicago, IL: University of Chicago Press.

Martin, Joanne (1990) 'Deconstructing organizational taboos: the suppression of gender conflict in organizations', *Organization Science,* 1 (4): 339–59.

McCloskey, D.N. (1985) *The Rhetoric of Economics.* Madison, WI: University of Wisconsin Press.

McCloskey, D.N. (1990a) *If You Are So Smart. The Narrative of Economic Expertise.* Chicago, IL: University of Chicago Press.

McCloskey, D.N. (1990b) 'Storytelling in economics', in Cristopher Nash (ed.) *Narrative in Culture. The Uses of Storytelling in the Sciences, Philosophy and Literature.* London: Routledge, 5–22.

McCloskey, D.N. (1994) *Knowledge and Persuasion in Economics.* New York, NY: Cambridge University Press.

McCloskey, D.N. (2000) *How to be Human**Though an Economist.* Ann Arbor, MI: University of Michigan Press.

Miller, Jody, and Glassner, Barry (1997) 'The "inside" and the "outside". Finding realities in interviews', in David Silverman (ed.) *Qualitative Research. Theory, Method and Practice.* London: Sage, 99–111.

Mintzberg, Henry (1991) 'A letter to Marta Calás and Linda Smircich', *Organization Studies,* 12 (4): 602.

Mintzberg, Henry (1999) 'Managing quietly', *Leader to Leader,* 12 (Spring): 24–30.

Mishler, Elliot G. (1986) *Research Interviewing. Context and Narrative.* Cambridge, MA: Harvard University Press.

Mitchell, W.J.T. (ed.) (1981) *On Narrative.* Chicago, IL: University of Chicago Press.

Mulkay, Michael (1985) *The Word and the World. Explorations in the Form of Sociological Analysis.* London: Allen & Unwin.

Mulkay, Michael, and Gilbert, G. Nigel (1982) 'Accounting for error: how scientists construct their social world when they account for correct and incorrect belief', *Sociology,* 16: 165–83.

Nagel, Thomas (1974) 'What is it like to be a bat?' *The Philosophical Review,* LXXXIII (4): 435–50.

Narayan, Kirin, and George, Kenneth M. (2002) 'Personal and folk narrative as cultural representation', in Jaber F. Gubrium and James A. Holstein (eds) *Handbook of Interview Research. Context and Method.* Thousand Oaks, CA: Sage, 815–32.

Nash, Christopher (ed.) (1990) *Narrative in Culture: The Uses of Storytelling in Sciences, Philosophy and Literature.* London: Routledge.

Nelson, John S., Megill, Allan, and McCloskey, Deirdre N. (eds) (1987) *The Rhetoric of the Human Sciences.* Madison, WI: University of Wisconsin Press.

New Encyclopædia Britannica, The (1990) Micropædia. Chicago, IL: University of Chicago Press.

Norris, Christopher (1988) 'Deconstruction, post-modernism and visual arts', in Christopher Norris, and Andrew Benjamin (eds) *What is Deconstruction?*. London: Academy Editions, 7–55.

Orr, Julian E. (1996) *Talking about Machines. An Ethnography of a Modern Job.* Ithaca, NY: Cornell University Press.

Overington, Michael A. (1977a) 'Kenneth Burke and the method of dramatism', *Theory and Society*, 4: 131–56.

Overington, Michael A. (1977b) 'Kenneth Burke as social theorist', *Sociological Inquiry*, 47 (2): 133–41.

Oxford English Dictionary, The New Shorter (1993) Oxford: Clarendon Press.

Pears, Iain (1998) *An Instance of the Fingerpost*. London: Vintage.

Polanyi, Karl (1944) *The Great Transformation. The Political and Economic Origins of our Time*. Boston, MA: Beacon Press.

Polkinghorne, Donald E. (1987) *Narrative Knowing and the Human Sciences.* Albany, NY: State University of New York Press.

Propp, Vladimir (1928/1968) *Morphology of the Folktale.* Austin, TX: University of Texas Press.

Psathas, George (1995) *Conversation Analysis: The Study of Talk-in-interaction.* Thousand Oaks, CA: Sage.

Rhodes, Carl (2001) *Writing Organization: (Re)Presentation and Control in Narratives at Work.* Amsterdam: John Benjamins.

Richardson, Laurel (1990) 'Narrative and sociology', *Journal of Contemporary Ethnography*, 19 (1): 116–35.

Ricoeur, Paul (1981) 'The model of the text: meaningful action considered as text', in John B. Thompson (ed. and trans.) *Hermeneutics and the Human Sciences*. Cambridge: Cambridge University Press, 197–221.

Ricoeur, Paul (1984) *Time and Narrative. Vol. 1*. Chicago, IL: University of Chicago Press.

Ricoeur, Paul (1986) *Time and Narrative. Vol. 2*. Chicago, IL: University of Chicago Press.

Riessman, Catherine Kohler (1993) *Narrative Analysis*. Newbury Park, CA: Sage.

Robichaud, Daniel (2003) 'Narrative institutions we organize by', in Barbara Czarniawska and Pasquale Gagliardi (eds) *Narratives We Organize by*. Amsterdam: John Benjamins, 37–54.

Robinson, G.D. (1995) 'Paul Ricoeur and the hermeneutics of suspicion: a brief overview and critique', *Premise*, II (8): 12.

Rorty, Richard (1980) *Philosophy and the Mirror of Nature*. Oxford: Blackwell.

Rorty, Richard (1989) *Contingency, Irony and Solidarity*. Cambridge: Cambridge University Press.

Rorty, Richard (1991) 'Inquiry as recontextualization: an anti-dualist account of interpretation', in Richard Rorty, *Philosophical Papers 1. Objectivity, Relativism and Truth*. New York, NY: Cambridge University Press, 93–110.

Rorty, Richard (1992) 'The pragmatist's progress', in Umberto Eco, *Interpretation and Overinterpretation*. Cambridge: Cambridge University Press, 89–108.

Ryan, Marie-Laure (1993) 'Narrative in real time: chronicle, mimesis and plot in baseball broadcast', *Narrative*, 1 (2): 138–55.

Sacks, Harvey (1992) *Lectures on Conversation*. Oxford: Blackwell.

Schank, Richard C., and Abelson, Robert (1977) *Scripts, Plans, Goals and Understanding.* Hillsdale, NJ: Lawrence Erlbaum Associates.

Scheytt, Tobias, Soin, Kim, and Metz, Thomas (2003) 'Exploring notions of control across cultures: a narrative approach', *European Accounting Review,* forthcoming.

Schütz, Alfred (1973) *Collected Papers. I. The Problem of Social Reality.* The Hague: Martinus Nijhoff.

Scott, Martin B., and Lyman, Stanford M. (1968) 'Accounts', *American Sociological Review,* 33: 46–62.

Seale, Clive, Giampietro Gobo, Jaber F. Gubrium and David Silverman (eds) (2003) *Qualitative Research Practice.* London: Sage.

Selden, Raman (1985) *A Reader's Guide to Contemporary Literary Theory.* Brighton: Harvester Press.

Sennett, Richard (1998) *The Corrosion of Character. The Personal Consequences of Work in the New Capitalism.* New York, NY: Norton.

Shotter, John, and Gergen, Kenneth J. (eds) (1989) *Texts of Identity.* London: Sage.

Silverman, David (1975) *Reading Castaneda: A Prologue to the Social Sciences.* London: Routledge & Kegan Paul.

Silverman, David (ed.) (1997) *Qualitative Research: Theory, Method, Practice.* London: Sage.

Silverman, David (2001) *Interpreting Qualitative Data. Methods for Analysing Talk, Text and Interaction* (2nd edn). London: Sage.

Silverman, David, and Jones, Jill (1976) *Organizational Work: The Language of Grading and the Grading of Language.* London: Collier Macmillan.

Silverman, David, and Torode, Brian (1980) *The Material Word. Some Theories About Language and Their Limits.* London: Routledge & Kegan Paul.

Silvers, Robert B. (ed.) (1995) *Hidden Histories of Science.* New York, NY: NYRB.

Simonen, Leila (1991) *Feminist Social Policy in Finland.* London: Avebury.

Simons, Herbert (ed.) (1988) *Rhetoric in the Human Sciences.* London: Sage.

Simons, Herbert (1990) *The Rhetorical Turn.* Chicago, IL: University of Chicago Press.

Sini, Carlo (ed.) (1992) *Filosofia (Dizionario).* Milano: Jaca Book.

Sköldberg, Kaj (1994) 'Tales of change: public administration reform and narrative mode', *Organization Science,* 5 (2): 219–38.

Sköldberg, Kaj (2002) *The Poetic Logic of Administration.* London: Routledge.

Smith, Dorothy E. (1987) *The Everyday World as Problematic: A Feminist Sociology.* Boston, MA: Northern University Press.

Smith, Dorothy E. (1990) *Texts, Facts, and Femininity. Exploring the Relations of Ruling.* London: Routledge.

Smith, Dorothy E. (1999) *Writing the Social. Critique, Theory and Investigations.* Toronto: University of Toronto Press.

Solow, Robert (1988) 'Comments from inside economics', in Arjo Klamer et al. (eds) *The Consequences of Economic Rhetoric.* Cambridge: Cambridge University Press, 31–7.

Søderberg, Anne-Marie (2003) 'Sensegiving and sensemaking in integration processes. A narrative approach to the study of an international acquisition', in Barbara Czarniawska and Pasquale Gagliardi (eds) *Narratives we Organize by.* Amsterdam: John Benjamins, 3–36.

Spradley, James P. (1979) *The Ethnographic Interview.* New York, NY: Holt, Rinehart & Winston.

Stiglitz, Joseph E. (2002) 'A fair deal for the world', *New York Review of Books*, XLIX (9): 24–8.

ten Have, Paul (1998) *Doing Conversation Analysis*. London: Sage.

Thompson, James D. (1967) *Organizations in Action: Social Science Bases of Administrative Theory*. New York, NY: McGraw-Hill.

Thompson, John B. (1981) 'Editor's introduction', in Paul Ricoeur, *Hermeneutics and the Human Sciences*. New York, NY: Cambridge University Press, 1–26.

Thompson, Paul (1978) *The Voice of the Past. Oral History*. Oxford: Oxford University Press.

Todorov, Tzvetan (1971/1977) *The Poetics of Prose*. Oxford: Blackwell.

Todorov, Tzvetan (1978/1990) *Genres in Discourse*. Cambridge: Cambridge University Press.

Turner, Victor (1982) *From Ritual to Theatre*. New York, NY: Performing Arts Journal Publications.

Van Fraassen, Bas C. and Sigman, Jill (1993) 'Interpretation in science and in the arts', in George Levine (ed.) *Realism and Representation: Essays on the Problem of Realism in Relation to Science, Literature and Culture*. Madison, WI: University of Wisconsin Press, 73–99.

Van Maanen, John (1988) *Tales of the Field*. Chicago, IL: University of Chicago Press.

Van Maanen, John (ed.) (1995) *Representation in Ethnography*. Thousand Oaks, CA: Sage.

Veyne, Paul (1988) *Did the Greeks Believe in their Myths?*. Chicago, IL: University of Chicago Press.

Waldo, Dwight (1968) *The Novelist on Organization and Administration*. Berkeley, CA: Institute of Government Studies.

Watson, Karen Ann (1973) 'A rhetorical and sociolinguistic model for the analysis of narrative', *American Anthropologist*, 75: 243–64.

Weick, Karl (1995) *Sensemaking in Organizations*. Thousand Oaks, CA: Sage.

White, Hayden (1973) *Metahistory. The Historical Imagination in Nineteenth Century Europe*. Baltimore, MD: Johns Hopkins University Press.

White, Hayden (1987) *The Content of the Form. Narrative Discourse and Historical Representation*. Baltimore, MD: Johns Hopkins University Press.

White, Hayden (1999) *Figural Realism*. Baltimore, MD: Johns Hopkins University Press.

Wolf, Margery (1992) *A Thrice-told Tale*. Stanford, CA: Stanford University Press.

Woolgar, Steve (1988) *Science: The Very Idea*. London: Tavistock.

Yanow, Dvora (1996) *How Does a Policy Mean? Interpreting Policy and Organizational Actions*. Washington, DC: Georgetown University Press.

Author Index

Subject Index

—